How To Use Games in Language Teaching

by Shelagh Rixon

Essential Language Teaching Series

General Editors: Roger H Flavell Monica Vincent

MODERN ENGLISH
PUBLICATIONS

Published 1996 by
Phoenix ELT
Campus 400, Spring Way
Maylands Avenue, Hemel Hempstead
Hertfordshire, HP2 7EZ
A division of Prentice Hall International

First published 1981 by Macmillan Publishers Ltd

Typeset by August Filmsetting, Reddish, Stockport

Printed and bound in Hong Kong

A catalogue record for this book is available from the British Library

ISBN 0 13 400326 8

12 11 10 9 8

99 98 97 96

Acknowledgements

Types of games form such a close network that probably no game described in this book will be without a precursor or near relative, even those I *think* I made up myself! Particular mention should be made of the work of Donn Byrne, Jim Kerr, Marion Geddes, Gill Sturtridge, and Janet McAlpin on the original corpus of games developed in the British Council's English Language Teaching Institute in London. Games such as *Describe and Draw, Describe and Arrange, Find Your Partner* and *Find the Difference* come from this source. Betty Morgan Bowen of The Bell College, Saffron Walden provided very helpful advice on the original manuscript and kindly allowed me to use games from her own book as illustrative material. Ros Levy's ideas on multi-purpose games materials are also acknowledged with thanks. My interest in the use of games in education and in the theory and practice of designing games to fit a purpose was greatly stimulated by the work and the teaching of G. I. Gibbs also to whom my thanks.

S. R.

Preface

This book is written for teachers by a teacher – one who has used language games herself and found them to be not only useful but popular as well. Many teachers will have already tried games successfully, but there must also be some who have not found the experience pleasant for themselves or instructive for their classes. Still others may be quite new to the idea and unsure whether it would be useful or practically possible with their students. I hope that the book will contain something for all three groups: new games for teachers who are already convinced, reassurance for those who have tried games and are doubtful of their success, and encouragement for those who have yet to try them.

This is not primarily a recipe book of classroom games, although more than thirty are described in the text, which I hope teachers will try. It is a book *about* games – how to choose suitable ones and how to organise them and use them so that students get the most language practice from them. Further games may be gleaned from the sources given at the end of the book.

Contents

1 Games and language teaching

There are hundreds of games that can be used in some connection with language teaching. In this book we shall be looking at ways in which they can be integrated with teaching so that they become a positive part of it rather than a time-filler or, worse, a time-waster.

An effective user of games in the language classroom is not necessarily the teacher who has a long list of them in his head, but someone who has really thought about them and knows their ingredients and how they can be varied to call forth different activities and skills from the players. A teacher who understands games in this way is much more likely to be able to find or create games that will help his students to learn something as they play.

The most obvious way of classifying games from a language teacher's point of view is according to the language they practise: listening games, spelling games, games to help students build vocabulary, games that bring in a structure or a function, and so on. Figure 1 groups some of the games mentioned in this book under headings like this.

Looking at the language skills involved is a good start when considering whether a particular game will be suitable for a particular purpose, but other features may be just as important. Does the game need the teacher or someone else to act as leader or master of ceremonies, for example, or can it be played by groups of students on their own? Are the players competing, and, if so, in teams or individually, or is it a game in which players can co-operate? Is it an active noisy game or one which can be played

i Main language skill involved

Spelling Hangman, How Many Words Can You Make?, Spelling Bee
Vocabulary The Minister's Cat, Vocabulary Bingo, Vocabulary Pelmanism, Vocabulary Snap, What's the Word?
Listening Comprehension If, O'Grady Says, Which One Is It?
Sound Discrimination Pronunciation Bingo, Ship or Sheep?
Reading Comprehension Do As You Are Told
Pronunciation Pronunciation Find Your Partner

ii Language functions needed

Giving and following instructions Describe and Arrange, Describe and Draw, Furnish the Room
Justification Gifts for the Family, If, Picture Dominoes
Expressing intention Picture Dominoes, Gifts for the Family
Agreement and disagreement If, Gifts for the Family, Picture Dominoes
Description Describe and Draw, Find the Difference, The Lego Game
Giving definitions What's the Word?

iii Structures and grammatical points practised

Question forms and short answers Botticelli, I Spy, What's in the Bag?, What's My Line?
'Is There?', 'There is', etc Find the Difference
'Have you got . . .?' Find Your Partner, Happy Families
'A . . . with . . .' Describe and Arrange, Find Your Partner, Which One Is It?
'What's the time . . .?', 'It's . . . o'clock' What's the Time, Mr Wolf?
Imperatives Describe and Arrange, Describe and Draw, Do As You Are Told, Furnish the Room, If, O'Grady Says
Second conditional If He Were a Flower
First and second conditional: 'Unless . . .', etc If
Prepositions Describe and Arrange, Furnish the Room
Past tenses Past Tense Bingo, Past Tense Knockout

Figure 1 Ways of categorising language games in this book

quietly sitting at desks? These and other factors make different games practically as well as pedagogically suitable for different circumstances.

But, first of all, what is a game? How do games and learning fit together? Looking at games in general, with examples from the everyday world as well as from games specially designed with teaching in mind, may help us to pick out features that will be useful in language teaching and to see what other features will be less useful or even a waste of time.

A game consists of play governed by rules. Kicking a ball around in the park is play: adding rules about how and where you can kick the ball and giving your efforts an objective (like getting it between two goalposts) turn this play into a game. This is summed up very well in Gibbs' definition (1978: p. 60) of a game as 'an activity carried out by cooperating or competing decision-makers, seeking to achieve, within a set of rules, their objectives'. Applying this to teaching, one can see how students playing a game are encouraged to use language to some purpose. The purpose may be an artificial one determined by the game, but the skills exercised to achieve that purpose may be applied in every day life just like the skills used in 'ordinary' games. These are many and varied: coordination of hand and eye in games like netball and tennis, memory in a game like pelmanism, tactics in draughts or chess. Whatever the game, the skills employed in it are developed and improved through the repeated use they get, and, most important, the players want to improve the skills necessary for a game they enjoy. Both these principles apply to language games too.

For language-teaching purposes we need to make sure that the skills needed in any game are heavily enough weighted on the language side. For example, chess is an excellent game in itself, but it is almost useless from the language-teaching point of view. The obvious reason is that players need not communicate with one another during the game – at least not with words. The skills used in chess are intellectual and tactical and not linguistic. This is an extreme example, but many other promising-looking and well-known games depend too little on the use of language to be at all useful to language learners without considerable adaptation.

Another thing that needs to be taken into consideration is the proportion of luck to skill in any game. A lot of the fun of many games comes from the unpredictable outcome of a throw or move or from the random dealing of cards, but the best games also allow players to use their skill to improve upon what chance brings them. Card games like bridge and whist are good everyday examples of this type of game. For the language classroom, a dash of luck in a game can make it more exciting and give the less able students a chance to catch up with their fellows for once, but a game that depends too much on luck and too little on use of language will waste students' time. The ideal combination is a game in which students have to react, by using language, to some challenge which may be decided by the luck of drawing a card or throwing a die, for example.

Games are closed activities. In other words they have a very clearly marked beginning and end. There is a definite point at which the game is over or has been 'won', and it is usually easy to see how near to that point the players are. One team is near the target score, for example, or someone has nearly finished all his cards or is close to the end of the board.

This closure is a very useful feature from the teacher's point of view. Because students know exactly when a game will be over or how close they are to finishing it, it helps to give some structure to what they are doing. It means that some games can run themselves with little organisational supervision from the teacher. This leaves him free to monitor students' performance and give them appropriate help on the language side. A well-designed game has its own momentum and is far less likely to 'run out of steam' than many other classroom activities. For pairs and small groups of students, games are often easier to keep going than even the best organised open-ended language-practice exercises.

The fact that all games have players may seem too obvious to mention, but if we compare the way in which players can be moved about and put into different relationships in different games with the ways in which a teacher may want to change the patterns within his class, the interesting possibilities offered by some games will become clear.

One of the main concerns of current methodology is how to vary what happens between students and teacher so that it goes beyond the classic teacher-to-whole-class pattern of interaction. The aim is often to get students talking to one another rather than always addressing their remarks to the teacher or having him mediate what they say to one another. All teachers must have had the experience of the student who refuses to look at anyone other than the teacher even when he is asked to say something to one of his classmates! Games that organise players into different patterns of interaction can help to break down such habits and inhibitions. Players can become so engrossed in a game that they forget to act in the classic classroom patterns and start to react directly to what their fellows are saying or doing. There is also, of course, a place for games in which the teacher leads the activity. Figure 2 shows some of the possibilities, and in Chapter 5 we shall be looking more closely at interaction patterns that suit different stages in a lesson.

The first thing that many people think of in connection with games is competition among players. This is a feature of many games, but there are some in which cooperation is the main thing. In other games there is both cooperation and competition – cooperation within a team and competition against another team, for example. The type of language use you wish to encourage may make you choose between cooperation or competition as the basis of players' relationships within a game (see Figure 3).

The actual language that is called for varies from game to game, but there is a basic division in what the students must do with it in order to achieve success. In some games the rules demand that a player should be formally correct in his handling of the language. For example, he must produce a structure correctly, pronounce or spell something correctly or recognise the difference between two sounds. Success in these things is judged, and marks or points are given accordingly. In other games success comes from conveying a message well enough for

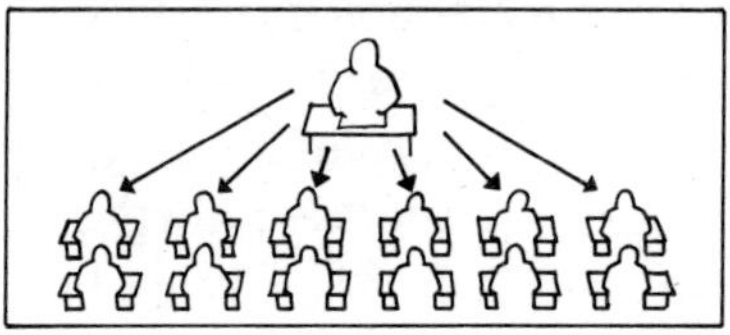

O'Grady Says
(leader challenging whole group)

Ship or Sheep?
(leader challenging members of two teams)

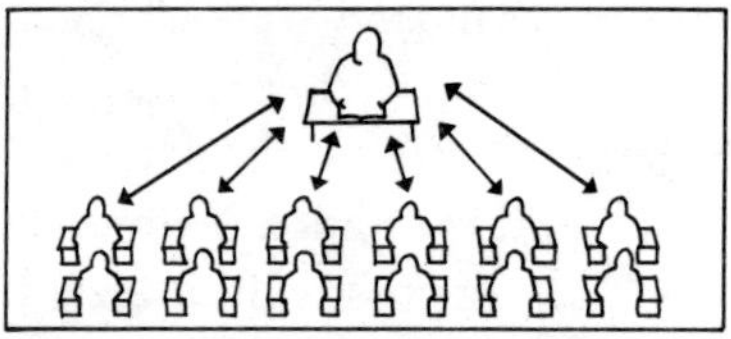

I Spy, What's My Line?
(leader challenging whole group, who can ask him questions)

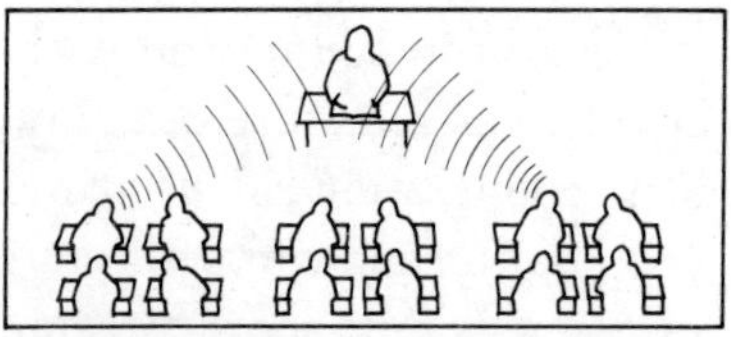

Describe and Draw
(pairs working together; teacher monitoring)

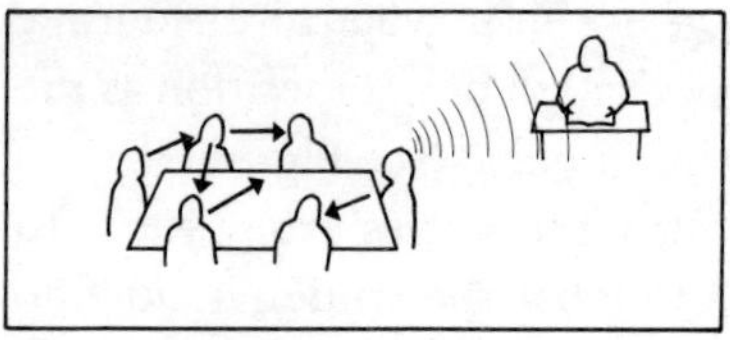

If, Gifts for the Family, Picture Dominoes
(small groups working together; teacher monitoring)

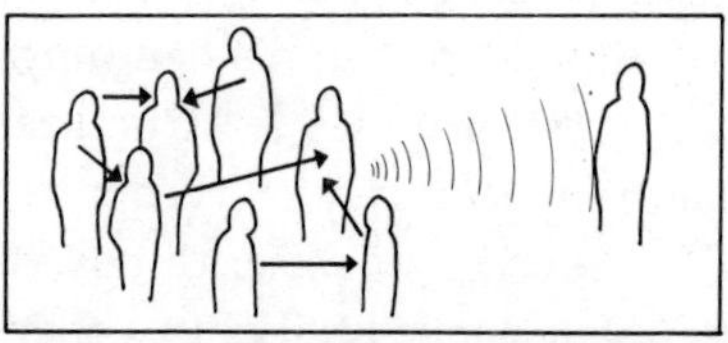

Find Your Partner
(everyone in class free to talk to everyone else)

Figure 2 The interactions set up by different games

<table>
<tr><th></th><th>Cooperative</th><th>Competitive</th></tr>
<tr><td>Grouping and interaction</td><td>Everyone together
Cooperating within a group, then with other groups</td><td>One person against the rest
Each person individually</td></tr>
<tr><td></td><td colspan="2">With a team against the rest
With a partner against the rest</td></tr>
<tr><td>Aim</td><td>Completing something
Reproducing an unseen drawing, etc
Putting things in order, eg stages of a story
Grouping things, eg similar pictures
Finding a pair, eg one's partner</td><td>Finishing first, eg using up cards, reaching end of board
Getting the most points, cards, etc
Surviving elimination
Avoiding penalties
Becoming challenger or 'he'
Avoiding becoming challenger or 'he'</td></tr>
<tr><td></td><td colspan="2">Finding something hidden, eg object in class
Solving a puzzle
Discovering a secret</td></tr>
<tr><td>Language functions required</td><td>Exchanging information
Giving and following instructions</td><td>Producing more formally correct language
Responding correctly to language more often
Questioning and extracting information more effectively
Drawing conclusions more quickly
Justifying a move successfully</td></tr>
<tr><td>Motivation</td><td>Information gap (see Index) between players to be bridged only by using language</td><td>Opinion gap (see Index) between players to be bridged by justifying moves
Challenge to get something right</td></tr>
</table>

Figure 3 Cooperative and competitive games compared

another player to understand it. One player may, for example, be trying to describe a picture well enough for another to be able to draw it, or be trying to persuade other players that there is some link between the two pictures that he wishes to place together as part of a move in the game. It is obvious that the range of language in this sort of game will be much greater than that found in the 'correctness' games, and that the likelihood of making some mistakes whilst carrying out these demanding operations will be high. Players will nevertheless succeed in reaching the objective of the game provided that their overall message is clear. In other words, the emphasis in this type of game is more upon successful communication than absolute correctness. The different uses of games for formal correctness and games for communicative effectiveness will be dealt with in more detail in Chapter 2.

The rest of this chapter looks at the rules of a number of games in more detail, both as a way of showing how many different forms language games can take without deviating from the basic characteristics outlined in the beginning of the chapter, and to illustrate some of the ways of assessing success and failure in a game.

The first game, *What's My Line?* (or, in other words, What's My Job?), should be familiar to many teachers. It is included here as an example of a simple question-and-answer game where there is no reliance on non-linguistic skills and where pure chance has no part to play. Logical deduction is important, but the information upon which the logic can work can only be gathered through use of language.

Questions and answers make up the whole game. It is played entirely through language and can therefore be expected to help students improve their command of the language. *What's My Line?* has another virtue from the teacher's point of view since it is easy to predict fairly accurately the range of language that the students will need in order to play it. Questions and answers – listening and replying – will make up most of the game. Because

WHAT'S MY LINE?

LEVEL Beginners, Intermediate — Oral/Aural

AGE 10 years to Adult

PLAYERS Challenger + Whole Class
or
Challenger + Competing Teams
Challenger + Small Group
Pairs

TIMING 2–3 minutes per turn

LOCATION Classroom

VOCABULARY earn, work, etc. and names of jobs.

MAIN LANGUAGE Present Simple Affirmative, Negative Question forms + Short Answers

DESCRIPTION The challenger thinks of a job or profession. The other players try to discover what it is by asking questions. They can only answer Yes/No questions like "Do you work indoors?" No WH- questions are allowed.

OPTIONS The number of questions can be limited to 20 after which the challenger has 'beaten the class.'

Teams can compete to see which can guess the job first. The person who guesses the job can take the place of the challenger, or players can take it in turn to challenge.

MATERIALS None essential, but pictures showing jobs and professions are useful as prompts to give challengers ideas.

of the topic of the game it is likely that the simple present will be the tense most often used, and verbs like 'work' and 'earn' will be obvious choices. It is easy to see where the game could fit into a course. In other words, the language points embedded in this game are clear and easy to define. Wherever possible, some indication of the language most likely to be elicited by each game described in this book is included. Another game in which language skills are exercised is *O'Grady Says,* but there is also a 'trick' element woven into the purely language-based part of the game to add to the fun without obscuring the main purpose.

O'Grady Says is a game in which players listen and react rather than producing any language of their own (except when acting as leader). They show their understanding by doing something. A student can be penalised for any mistake in his understanding, such as putting up his right hand when 'O'Grady' tells him to put up his left. The additional 'trick' element comes in the rule which says that he must only obey when 'O'Grady' tells him to do something. Even the best students are going to be caught out by this sometimes so that it has the effect of evening up everyone's chances. Devices like this or a judicious mixture of non-linguistic skills like fast running or catching a ball can help to keep up the interest, especially in classes where students are of different abilities. Language should, however, always be the basis of the game, as it is here.

Rewards and penalties within a game both keep the interest of the players high and give them some feedback on the success they are having in their use of language. The remaining games in this chapter illustrate different rewards and penalties that can be built into the play.

CHANGING PLACES

A frequent reward or penalty is for one player to take the place of another. In the many games based on 'tag' or 'he', for example, one player tries to catch or touch any of the others. When a

O'GRADY SAYS

LEVEL Beginners

AGE Best with children 6–12

PLAYERS Leader + whole class
leader + competing teams
leaders + small groups

TIMING Each instruction takes a few seconds. 5–10 minutes is the best length for the whole game.

LOCATION Classroom or playground.

Aural (listening to instructions)

MAIN LANGUAGE Imperatives

VOCABULARY: Parts of the body, action verbs (put, shake, lift, etc)

DESCRIPTION Leader gives instructions. Players obey him only if he says "O'Grady says....." — but take no notice if he gives instruction without saying this. Players who make a mistake are penalised.

eg. "O'Grady says put your right hand on your head" (everyone obeys)
"Touch your nose" (no one should obey)

OPTIONS Penalties: a black mark for player or his team.
being eliminated from the game.
changing places with "O'Grady" (+ Being laughed at)

MATERIALS None required

WHAT'S THE TIME, MR WOLF?

<u>LEVEL</u> Beginners
<u>AGE</u> Children
<u>PLAYERS</u> One "wolf" + 5 or more players
<u>TIMING</u> 5 – 10 minutes is enough for the whole game. 20 – 30 seconds for each turn.
<u>LOCATION</u> Gym hall or playground.

Oral/Aural + running around
<u>MAIN LANGUAGE</u>
What's the time..?
It's ....o'clock.
It's {dinner / lunch / breakfast} time!

<u>DESCRIPTION</u> Two circles are chalked on the floor, at least 30 ft apart. One small one is the wolf's lair, the larger one is the safe refuge for the players or 'sheep', but it is too small for all the sheep to fit into it. The wolf must stand in his lair, while the sheep circle him, saying in chorus "What's the time, Mr Wolf?" The wolf can answer "It's one o'clock, it's two o'clock" etc in which case he must stay in his lair, but after 5 questions have been asked he can add wherever he chooses. "... and it's {lunchtime / dinnertime / tea time} etc" Then he can come out of his lair and try to catch one of the sheep for his meal. The sheep run back to their refuge, but since it is not big enough for them all, the wolf is sure to catch someone. The captured sheep becomes the new wolf.

<u>MATERIALS:</u> Chalk for circles, and plenty of space.

player is caught he takes the place of 'he' and has to wait for his chance to catch someone else, who in turn will become 'he'. *What's The Time, Mr Wolf?* is an example of this type of game with a language element built in. Both sides repeat formulaic language until the 'wolf' decides to start chasing the 'sheep', but before he can do this he must give a different response to their question, which should warn them to start running!

Changing roles can be a reward in other games. In *I Spy,* players compete to become the next challenger by being the first person to guess the answer to the puzzle.

ELIMINATING PLAYERS

In some games unsuccessful players are eliminated so that the winner is the one who survives the longest. *O'Grady Says* can be played in such a way that any player who makes a mistake goes 'out'. A variation is to give each player a number of 'lives' which allow him to make some mistakes until he loses all his lives and is finally out.

COLLECTING AND GETTING RID OF THINGS

Very often this type of game consists of a race to get rid of all one's cards or pieces, as in *Dominoes,* to collect a complete set of cards or pieces, as in *Happy Families,* or to win all one's opponent's pieces, as in *Draughts* or *Snap*. This type of procedure is an excellent one to adopt for language games. In the next two games – *Picture Dominoes* and *Gifts for the Family* – trying to acquire or get rid of a card gets the players arguing and discussing.

In *Picture Dominoes,* because the pictures have no obvious links between them, it is up to each player to use his imagination and ingenuity to find one. Figure 4 shows some examples of cards and the links that might be made between each pair. Because this is a competitive game, the players are almost sure to argue about whether the links made are plausible or not, and the teacher may have to arbitrate (see Section 4.4). Communication

I SPY or WHAT CAN YOU SEE?

LEVEL Beginners, Intermediate — Oral/Aural

AGE Children to Adult

PLAYERS Challenger + group
Challenger + competing teams

TIMING 1–2 minutes for each turn

LOCATION Classroom

MAIN LANGUAGE Yes/No questions + answers

DESCRIPTION The challenger thinks of an object in the room. In the traditional game he says "I spy with my little eye - something beginning with A, B, S" etc as appropriate.

The players ask him Yes/No questions to help them guess what the object is.

OPTIONS Scores can be given according to the number of questions it takes to get the right answer. Penalties can be given for wrong guesses. The player to guess correctly could take the place of the challenger.

MATERIALS: None

takes place as a result of a conflict of interests – each player's determination to get rid of more domino cards than anyone else.

In *Gifts for the Family* the aim is to collect gift cards rather than to get rid of them, but the principle is the same: players must argue in order to achieve what they want.

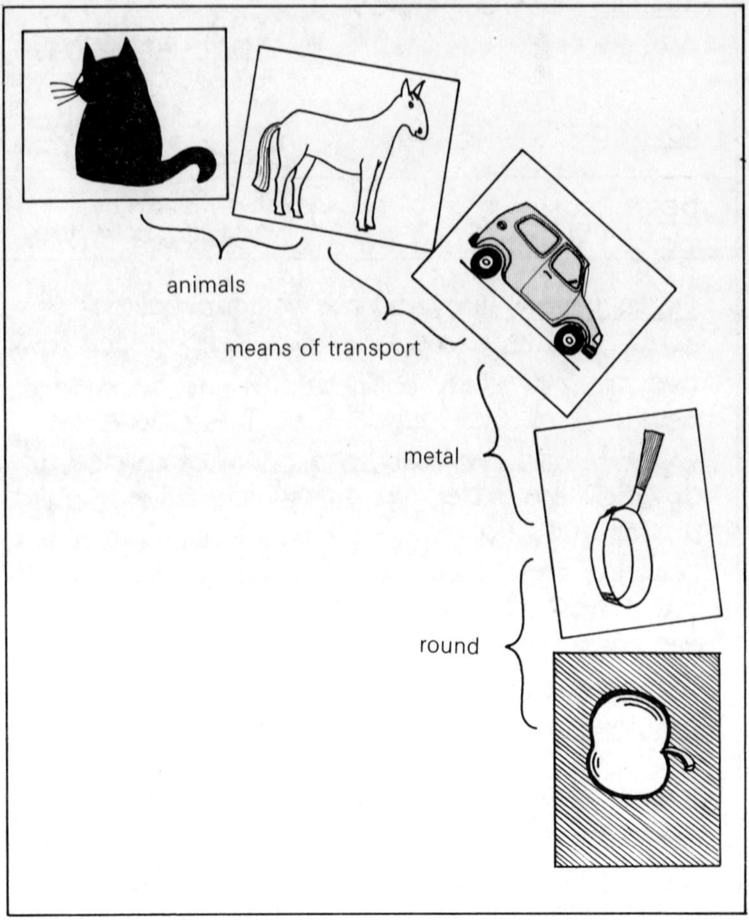

Figure 4 Some picture dominoes

PICTURE DOMINOES

LEVEL Intermediate to Advanced Oral/Aural
AGE Children to Adults
PLAYERS Small group, 3–6
TIMING 10–15 minutes

MAIN LANGUAGE
Agreement/Disagreement
Justification
based on comparison
of 2 things
neither, both, too

DESCRIPTION Players have an equal number of small picture cards, which they keep hidden from one another. They compete with one another to get rid of all their cards first. This is done by trying to add one card to a chain of cards laid down on the table, as in dominoes. The pictures are all different, and players must find a link between their own card and the one they want to put it next to. They must explain this link to the other players, who decide whether to accept the explanation or not.
OPTIONS 1/. Total no. of cards held by players, at least 6, but more are possible for a longer game. 2/. Players may be allowed to put down more than 1 card at a time if they can find the links. MATERIALS: Small uniformly sized cards with different pictures stuck or drawn on.

GIFTS FOR THE FAMILY

<u>LEVEL</u> Intermediate to Advanced

<u>AGE</u> Teenage to Adult

<u>PLAYERS</u> Groups of 4–6

<u>TIMING</u> 10–15 minutes

<u>LOCATION</u> Classroom

Oral/Aural

<u>MAIN LANGUAGE</u> Justification Disagreement/Agreement

<u>VOCAB</u> "Suitable for" + names of objects & members of the family.

<u>DESCRIPTION</u> Each player takes a FAMILY CARD with a description of a relative on it eg. "An elderly uncle who likes gardening, and hates dogs and children" or "A small boy aged 3". Players take it in turns to pick up one GIFT CARD from the central pack. Their aim is to collect as many GIFTS for their relative as possible, but they can only keep a GIFT card if they can justify to the other players giving the object shown on it to their relative. eg. the elderly uncle would not like to receive a puppy but might like a garden spade. When all the cards have been claimed, or after a time-limit, or a fixed number of rounds, the player with the most GIFT CARDS is the winner.

<u>MATERIALS</u> A set of varied descriptions of relatives or friends. A set of about 30 picture cards showing possible gifts.

IF

LEVEL Intermediate to Advanced
AGE Teenage to Adult
PLAYERS Groups of 4-6
TIMING 15 minutes
LOCATION Classroom

Oral/Aural (with some reading aloud)

MAIN LANGUAGE Conditionals, Justification, Agreement/Disagreement

DESCRIPTION Players are competing to reach the end of a track on a board. Each space on the track has a picture of an object or a living creature in it. Players move by following instructions read to them by another player. These instructions are on small cards kept in a pack in the centre of the table.
eg. of an instruction - "Move forward 10 if you are on a square showing something dangerous. If not go back 3."
Players are motivated to interpret "their square" in a way that allows them to go forward. They must justify this to the other players.

MATERIALS Board with a track of about 60 squares each with a small picture on it. Set of about 30 instruction cards. Small tokens to mark players' progress around the board.

GETTING SOMEWHERE FIRST

Another type of race is one that happens in many board games. Players compete to see who can reach the Finish square first. In some well-known board games like Snakes and Ladders, this is almost entirely a matter of luck since moves depend on the throw of a die. For language-learning games, successful moves must depend on language rather than on luck. This happens in the board game *If*: here, players have to read instructions to one another and interpret them to their advantage, and each move must be justified to the other players. Figure 23 on page 110–111 shows how a game like this can be made.

FINDING SOMEONE OR SOMETHING

A race to find someone or something within the class is another device that gets students to use language. The first example, *Where Is It?*, gives players practice in reading instructions and passing information to other players.

Find Your Partner is a game that can be adapted to practise many different language points. The basic idea is that each player must look for a partner who has got an identical word or picture to his own. The players may not look at each other's cards but must find out who their partners are by talking to one another. This is the opposite of the situation in elimination games, in which everyone starts 'in' and gradually drops 'out': in *Find Your Partner* everyone starts 'out' and gradually becomes 'in' as players find their partners.

This chapter has been mainly concerned with showing how many options there are within games. Players, groupings, objectives, penalties, rewards and rules about language use can all be adjusted in some way; games do not all require two teams and a scorer! The following chapters describe how to choose suitable games and how to find the easiest and most effective ways of using them.

WHERE IS IT?

LEVEL Beginners to Intermediate

AGE Children

PLAYERS A group of 10-15, teacher as master of ceremonies

TIMING 5-10 minutes

LOCATION Classroom with desks moved out of the way

Reading and Oral/Aural

MAIN LANGUAGE Prepositions, language of location, Imperatives.

DESCRIPTION The teacher hides 3 or 4 small objects around the classroom. eg. a particular book can be hidden in a desk, a key can be put on top of a cupboard. He also puts some written clues around the walls. The players compete to see who can locate all the objects first. When an object has been spotted the player should not touch it but should go away and write down where it is. The written clues say things like "Now look on the windowsill." The clue on the windowsill might say "The key is somewhere near the blackboard" and so on. Players can cooperate and swap information if they think this is to their advantage.

MATERIALS Small objects. Set of about 10 written clues on small pieces of paper or card.

FIND YOUR PARTNER

LEVEL Beginners to Intermediate — Oral/Aural

AGE Children to Adult

PLAYERS Any even number from 6 upwards

TIMING About 5 minutes

MAIN LANGUAGE eg. Have you got...? I've got....... Is there a.... in your picture?

VOCAB Depends on pictures on the cards.

DESCRIPTION Each player is given one card which he is not allowed to show to anyone else. Every card has one exactly similar "partner" card. Players have to go round questioning each other about their cards, each player trying to find his partner. When 2 partners have found each other they stand on one side. The game ends when everyone has found his partner.

MATERIALS Picture cards showing similar objects eg. stick figures, houses, fruit etc. Every card has a matching duplicate. Cards should vary slightly in the number and positioning of the objects shown on them so that players will have to question one another closely to find out if a card matches theirs or not.

2 Correctness and communicative effectiveness

A distinction was made in Chapter 1 between games whose main focus is on correctness and those in which it is on communicative effectiveness. This distinction is not, of course, confined to games. These two themes in language teaching and learning run through everything a teacher does. It is not a question of having one or the other. We aim to achieve both correctness and communicative effectiveness with our students, but different teaching techniques are more appropriate for each and have to be done at different times – drills and controlled exercises to help correctness, and opportunities for freer expression to enable students to communicate more fluently and confidently. In just the same way, different types of game are appropriate for different purposes.

2.1 Code-control games

These games depend upon players producing correct language or demonstrating that they have interpreted a particular piece of language correctly. The length of each utterance is usually limited in this type of game – often one word only, and seldom longer than a sentence or two. Correct repetition of a limited range of language is the important thing in these games. In this way they are similar in their function to drills.

Just as with a drill, someone must judge the correctness of responses. The teacher is usually the only person with sufficient command of the target language to do this, so it follows that most of these games must be controlled or at least led by the teacher, who awards credit for correct answers and rejects incorrect ones.

In competitive games it is usually convenient to divide the class into teams. In aural/oral games players usually answer one at a time. There can be a fixed order for answering to make sure that everyone has a turn, or, in a more spontaneous game, players can attract the teacher's attention if they wish to answer. In this case it is important that a few players do not dominate. Some listening games allow a whole team to answer at once by silently signalling their choice of answer. The teacher can judge whether the majority decision is the correct one or not and award or withhold points accordingly. Pencil-and-paper games allow students to cooperate within teams and present a joint answer at the end in competition with other teams, or else they can work on their own, competing against everyone else in the class.

A good example of a code-control game is the sound-discrimination game often called *Ship or Sheep?* (although of course sounds other than the /ɪ/ and the /i/ of words like 'ship' and 'sheep' can be contrasted in the game).

Hangman is a well known spelling game. The code-control training comes in here because, as the overall pattern of each word becomes clearer, players should be making intelligent guesses based upon their knowledge of the spelling conventions of the language in question.

Players can also be required to say something correctly, sometimes to practise a structure, or to extend vocabulary and challenge memory as in 'list' games like *I Went Shopping*. Here the students have to speak in turn, and any player to make a mistake in the sentence is eliminated from the game. The list gets longer, and the task harder, and when only one student is left in the game, he is the winner.

Ways of winning and ways of organising students may vary in these games, but their underlying principle is the same: players must get things right in order to win.

SHIP OR SHEEP?

LEVEL Beginners to Advanced
AGE Children to Adult
PLAYERS One caller and competing teams
TIMING 5 minutes is enough
LOCATION Classroom

Aural/Sound discrimination

MAIN LANGUAGE minimal pairs as appropriate to students' needs eg /I/ vs /i/ or /p/ vs /b/

DESCRIPTION The caller says one of a pair of words distinguished by only one sound, eg. "ship" or "sheep" "bin" or "pin." Players indicate which word they think he said, one point for each correct answer. There should be visual cues so that this can be easily done. 2 pictures or flash cards with the 2 words should be shown as the caller says the word. Players could point to the card they think is correct, or else make a signal to show which sound they think they heard, eg. hands on heads for i: hands on desks for I

OPTIONS One member of each team can answer in turn, or the whole team can signal silently as above and the teacher take the majority answer.

MATERIALS Picture cards to cue students if they are to signal by pointing.

HANGMAN

Spelling

LEVEL Intermediate to Advanced

AGE 10 years to Adult

PLAYERS Challenger + whole class
Challenger + competing teams
Challenger + small group
Pairs

TIMING 2 – 5 minutes each challenge

LOCATION Classroom

MAIN LANGUAGE POINTS develops awareness of acceptable letter sequences in English words
names of letters of the alphabet

DESCRIPTION The challenger draws a number of dashes corresponding to the number of letters in a word that he has secretly thought of. The other players call out suggestions of what letters may be in the word. If they are correct the challenger writes in the letters. If they are wrong he draws in part of the scaffold or the hanged man. (The stages in the drawing are like this: ) The aim is to try to guess the word before the drawing is complete. If players fail the challenger can have another turn. When someone succeeds he takes the place of the challenger.

OPTIONS If the traditional drawing is too gruesome or frightening other scoring methods could be substituted eg. the word must be guessed within 10 suggestions.

MATERIALS Blackboard + chalk or pencil + paper.

I WENT SHOPPING

LEVEL Intermediate to Advanced
AGE Children to Adult
PLAYERS One group, 8 players upwards + arbiter
TIMING 5 – 10 minutes
LOCATION classroom

Oral/Aural + memory

MAIN LANGUAGE POINTS
I went.....
I bought...
vocabulary as introduced by players

DESCRIPTION The players speak in turn. If possible they should be in a circle, standing up at first, but when a player is eliminated he must sit down. The last player left standing is the winner.

The first player starts by saying "I went shopping and I bought a ......" The second repeats the sentence but adds one item and so on, so that the list gets longer and longer. As soon as a player makes any mistake in the list he is eliminated. The player after him then starts a new list. The game continues until only one player is left.

OPTIONS You can limit the type of item to go on the list – foodstuffs, clothing etc, or you can allow any item, even fantastic ones.

MATERIALS None

2.2 Communication games

In this type of game the emphasis is not so much on absolute correctness as on the overall message of players' language. Can they give a clear description, or can they follow a set of instructions, for example? Success is judged by the outcome of what is said rather than by its form. However, it should not be thought that communication games do not improve correctness: firstly, language that is too distorted by mistakes will fail to communicate anything, and secondly, the range of language needed in many of these games can be limited so that students are repeating structures many times.

A good example of a communication game is *Describe and Draw*. The main rule in this game is the one that forbids player B to see the original picture before the end of the game. This means that the only way he can find out about it is by having a conversation with A. The language used as the two sides try to solve the problem will be much freer and more varied than that used in a code-control game. When the game is over the objective will have been achieved by effective communication more than by absolutely perfect use of language.

In *Happy Families,* repeated, almost formulaic, language is used communicatively.

Beginners may like to have a cue sheet by them which not only lists the vocabulary items contained on each card but also sets out a sample question-and-answer exchange. Players do not have to stick to this, but the weaker ones can use it as a prop when necessary. The cue sheet could look something like this:

A Have you got . . . ?
B Yes, I have. / No, I haven't.
A Can I have it, please?
or
A Can I have . . ., please?
B No, I'm sorry. I haven't got it.

DESCRIBE AND DRAW

LEVEL Beginners to Advanced (depending on pictures used) — Oral/Aural + drawing

AGE Children to Adult

PLAYERS 1 Describer and a group of drawers
2 small teams
pairs

MAIN LANGUAGE Descriptive language particularly Location + relative position vocabulary depends on picture

TIMING 3 minutes upwards for each drawing depending on complexity of picture and accuracy aimed at by players.

DESCRIPTION 1 side (A) has a picture, which the other side (B) is not allowed to see. A describes the picture and B asks questions so that B can try to produce a sketch as similar as possible to A's original. The 2 pictures are compared at the end of the game to see how close B was able to come to the original.

OPTIONS A can watch B and correct any mistakes in his drawing or Neither A nor B should see the other's picture.

MATERIALS Pictures with easily drawn objects, or geometrical figures. Pencils, paper and erasers for B.

HAPPY FAMILIES

LEVEL Beginners to Intermediate

AGE Children to Adult (depending on context of the cards)

PLAYERS Small group, 4–6

TIMING 5–10 minutes

LOCATION Classroom

Oral/Aural + memory training

MAIN LANGUAGE

Have you got . . . ?

Can I have . . . please?

Yes I have/No I haven't,

No, I haven't got it

DESCRIPTION A pack of cards containing 'families' of 4 cards which go together is dealt among the players.

Players are trying to collect complete 'families' of 4 cards. They do this by taking it in turns to ask any other player if they have a particular card. If the answer is 'Yes' the asking player captures the card and has another turn. If he gets the answer 'No' he loses his turn. (Players must tell the truth!) When a player has no cards left he drops out of the game. The player who collects the most 'families' is the winner.

MATERIALS Traditional Happy Families packs can be bought, or home-made sets with different things on the cards can be made, eg. sets of 4 fruit, 4 vegetables, 4 drinks etc. A cue sheet can be used to help beginners with their questions and answers.

Many communication games can be played at any level of language and are good games even for native speakers. *Find the Difference* is very good for practising structures like 'I can see . . .', 'Can you see . . .?', 'Is there a . . . in your picture?', 'There's a . . . in my picture', etc.

In a communication game, the language used by the players may be formally less than perfect, but if the message is understood the objective will be reached. The students can measure their own success by the speed and efficiency with which they reach the objective of the game. This is very often done by making a visual comparison at the end of the game, as in *Describe and Draw* or *Find the Difference*. Because success or failure is so practically demonstrated, there is less onus on the teacher to give approval or to comment at every moment of the lesson. He drops his role as director of activities and becomes more of a monitor and language informant. Chapter 4 looks at this in more detail.

In many communication games there is some gap or disparity in the information the players have at the beginning of the game. Players have to use language to bridge this gap and get the information they need to complete the activity. This 'information gap' exists in *What's My Line?*, in which the players must question the challenger to find out what his job is. In *Find Your Partner* they ask questions to find out what is on the other people's cards. In *Describe and Draw* an unseen picture is drawn from instructions or a description given by another player.

By contrast, in games like *Picture Dominoes* and *Gifts for the Family* there is no difference in the information available to the players, as everyone can see all the cards on the table. The difference lies in the way in which the players choose to interpret the cards. Because games like this are competitive, everyone will be motivated to interpret the cards differently to suit themselves, so that there is bound to be a clash of opinion, which will lead to discussion. This 'opinion gap' is what lies behind the type of argument that occurs in these games.

FIND THE DIFFERENCE

LEVEL Beginners to Advanced
AGE 10 to Adult
PLAYERS In pairs
TIMING 3-5 minutes for each pair of pictures
LOCATION Classroom

Oral/Aural
MAIN LANGUAGE
"Have you got ..."
"I've got ....."
"Can you see ..."
etc.
+ language of description and location

DESCRIPTION Each player takes 1 of a pair of pictures. The pictures are similar but not identical. Players may not look at each other's pictures. By describing their own picture and asking questions about the other player's picture they must find a number of differences. When they have reached this number they may then look at each other's pictures and discuss any other differences they can see.
MATERIALS Pairs of pictures (advertisements are a good source, or simple line drawings for beginners) similar but not identical.

Because of this use of language to close a 'gap', the length of utterances in communication games is not so limited or predictable as it is in code-control games. Players will continue talking until they have achieved their objectives. Turn-taking in speech is negotiated among the players themselves rather than controlled by the teacher, and interruption and overtalking occur frequently. In this way students are given the chance to develop the skills needed for taking part in discussion as well as to practise individual language items.

Another way in which communication games differ from code-control games is that in a communication game there is always more than one way to reach the objective. In a game like *Find the Difference*, for example, players may adopt very different tactics. One pair may proceed by each player giving a description of his picture, with the other commenting on any differences he notices. Another pair may ask each other questions. This scope for individuality is another way in which the language used in communication games comes closer to the type of language students should eventually be able to use in real life.

The two types of game are not in conflict. Each has its place on a teaching programme (see Figure 5). Ideally, students will be able to use the correct language promoted by the code-control games in the flexible and effective way encouraged by communication games.

	Code-control games	Communication games
Main language focus	Getting language formally correct, ie structures, spelling, pronunciation, sound-discrimination, etc	Getting a message over to other players and reacting appropriately to their messages, ie giving and following instructions, describing something, persuading someone, etc
Aim	To score more points than or to win an advantage over other players by getting language correct	To achieve something—usually to complete a practical task, eg following instructions to build a model or draw a picture, or persuading other players to let one do something
Teaching advantages	Players are motivated by the game to concentrate on correct use of language Often an amusing extension of or alternative to drills and other formal exercises	Players can see the practical results of their use of language, so can evaluate their own success Successful completion of the task builds confidence Players have to stretch themselves and experiment with the language in order to get a point over Players are often less self-conscious because they are concentrating on the task rather than on the language

Figure 5 Code-control and communication games compared

3 Which games for which students?

Games can be used with a very wide range of students. They are not just for children and beginners. To back up this assertion I am going to describe some groups with whom I know that games have been used successfully. They may not be exactly similar to your students, but they may have enough in common with them to spark off ideas in your own mind.

The key to making games acceptable to any group of students is suitability. The descriptions which follow are intended to illustrate how different types of games were chosen to suit the language needs and the personalities of each group.

3.1 Children and young adolescents (lower intermediate/remedial)

In a Birmingham immigrant education centre I taught a class of about sixteen exuberant and sometimes downright naughty Bangladeshi boys aged from nine to sixteen. The education they had had before coming to England had accustomed them to the teacher directing most activities. The energy involved in keeping control of the class during work that was not directly led by me made me follow this teacher-led approach most of the time for reasons of pure survival! On the other hand, I wanted the boys to be as actively involved as my nerves would stand, and playing games was one of the ways of giving them this involvement. Games in which the teacher was the leader or the master of ceremonies were the safest from the discipline point of view.

Since the boys were learning English in England and having to use it every day outside the classroom, they had become reasonably fluent and confident in many areas, but their use of English remained very inaccurate in a formal sense. Running repairs were needed on this fluent but inaccurate English, especially where pronunciation was concerned. Teacher-led games were best here, too, because they were mostly competitive games in which points were given for correct language. The boys could thereby be made sensitive to distinctions they would not otherwise have bothered with.

While they were playing games they were strongly motivated towards correctness by their extreme competitiveness, which came at least partly from their earlier education. Each student would do his best to produce the language that would win his team a point, and each side would listen intently for a slip by the other side and appeal indignantly if they thought the teacher was being too generous.

Another characteristic of these students was a strong desire for the teacher's approval. This made them much keener to take part in activities like team games in which the teacher evaluates every answer than in the more independent pair or group games in which the teacher only occasionally listens in to each student. All in all, games like *What's My Line?*, *Ship or Sheep?*, and *What's in the Bag?* were the most successful.

These students also needed as much writing and spelling practice as possible. Contests like *Spelling Bee* were very popular with them.

Competition motivated them, but it was competition in a non-threatening atmosphere. Turning any of these games into a disguised test would have ruined the relationship between teacher and class.

There was also room for cooperation amongst students. There are many spelling and vocabulary games in which a small group can work together, although they are in competition with the rest

WHAT'S IN THE BAG?

LEVEL Beginners to Intermediate — Aural/Oral

AGE Children to Adult

PLAYERS One challenger + group of players
One challenger + competing teams of players
Pairs

TIMING 1–2 minutes for each turn

MAIN LANGUAGE
Yes/No questions
Yes it is/No it isn't

DESCRIPTION The challenger has a bag in which he hides an object, and asks the players "What's in the bag?" Players ask him questions about it "Is it heavy?" "Is it expensive?" etc. until they guess what it is.

OPTIONS 1 Scores can be given according to how many questions it takes the players before they get the right answer.

2 The first team or player to get the answer can win a point.

3 The player who guesses right is allowed to take the place of the challenger.

MATERIALS Paper or cloth bag. Collection of small objects kept hidden – sugar lumps, pencils, stones, apples etc.

N.B. Make sure that the challenger doesn't see all the objects or he will have an advantage later in the game!

SPELLING BEE

LEVEL Beginners to Advanced
AGE Children to Adults
PLAYERS Whole class in 2 teams
teacher master of ceremonies
TIMING 5 – 10 minutes
LOCATION Classroom

Spelling – conducted orally

MAIN LANGUAGE
Words from class vocabulary list

DESCRIPTION The two teams stand up to begin the game. The teacher reads a word to one member of the first team. The player must spell it correctly. If he fails he must sit down and the word passes to the other team. If it is spelled correctly the teacher reads out another word. Teams take it in turns to start. The game ends when the whole of one team has been eliminated, and they are all sitting down.

of the class. A good example of this is the spelling game *How Many Words Can You Make?*

In a mixed-ability class such as this it was far more productive to have groups of students working together than to have individual students struggling without much hope of being among the winners. With the right class atmosphere, students within each group will share the knowledge that they have and will query each other's ideas – about the correct spelling of a word, for example – as they try to amass more words than the other groups. In the follow-up stage after the word collection is over, each

HOW MANY WORDS CAN YOU MAKE?

LEVEL Intermediate to Advanced
AGE Teenager to Adult
PLAYERS Group or whole class competing individually with one another. Small groups competing against other groups.
TIMING 15–20 minutes
LOCATION Classroom

Spelling
MAIN LANGUAGE acceptable words derived from the letters in a longer word. Using a dictionary to check possible words.

DESCRIPTION A fairly long word eg. 'Dictionary' or 'Surprising' is put up on the blackboard. Players try to make as many other words as they can, using any of the letters in that word. They may not use any letter more often than it occurs in the original word (eg. 'Dictionary' has 2 "i"s so the new words may contain 1 or 2, but not 3 "i"s.)

OPTIONS The winner may be judged by the total number of words alone or, extra points may be awarded to players who find a word that no other player finds.

MATERIALS Blackboard and chalk, Pencil and paper for players.

group displays its findings and the teacher can collect all the words on the board. In this way the class can share any new words that they were not all able to find, and the group with the new word gains the credit. With oral group work it is possible for some students to feel abandoned by the teacher, but this does not happen when each group's results are written down as a demonstrable record of its achievement.

Games that involved running around in response to words of command were also popular with these very active students and gave them good training in listening skills. Much enjoyable language work could be built into their physical training lessons. Games like *What's the Time, Mr Wolf?* were much enjoyed.

The games played with these boys were useful linguistically because they concentrated on areas where their command of English could be improved in about the only ways that we could interest them in formal accuracy – through enjoyment and competition.

3.2 Young adults (lower intermediate to intermediate)

The young women in question were undergraduates from eighteen to twenty-six years old in the first year of their medical studies at a Middle Eastern university. There were about eighteen in a class, but occasionally two classes were taken together.

The whole of their university course was to be conducted in English, which they had all studied for about four years at secondary school. They needed to be able to follow lectures and read books on the physics, chemistry and biology that took up most of their pre-medical year. This was not the only purpose for which they needed English, however: they had to be able to communicate fluently with the largely English-speaking staff on everyday welfare and administrative matters as well as ask questions in lectures and laboratory sessions. Oral fluency was necessary both academically and socially, and in the science laboratories, being able to understand and ask for clarification of instructions was also a matter of safety.

Most of the girls were extremely efficient learners – new language would be committed to memory with almost alarming rapidity – but they needed help in making this knowledge active, especially orally. The best method of doing this seemed to be to set up practical activities that required the use of both technical and everyday language. For this reason, communication games were an important part of the course.

Like many teachers I was at first cautious about introducing games to this type of student because of their very serious attitude to their studies and because of the expectation that the teacher should behave in a generally authoritative way. However, I found that their attitude proved to be an advantage: they were prepared to believe that the teacher knew best and were happy to try out what was suggested. Because we started off with games requiring language that they had learned recently, they could see for themselves the benefit of what they were doing, and in time they were ready to try activities needing a wider range of language.

As a preparation for the sort of discussion the girls would have to cope with later on in their university studies, they were given puzzles and tasks to be solved in pairs or small groups. Students had to exchange information or cross-question each other in order to get explanations or clear instructions about what to do next. Getting the message over was the main aim, with the teacher on hand to monitor and help. These students were older, more mature and thus more capable of working by themselves than the Bangladeshi boys, so that it was not necessary to monitor every response and give approval at every moment. This type of independent yet structured pair and group work was thus quite appropriate to these students.

Many of the games were derived from exercises in the textbook we were using (*Nucleus General Science* by Martin Bates and Tony Dudley-Evans – Longman), which meant a high degree of integration with the rest of the teaching. To accompany the unit to do with describing location, for example, the students played a version of *Describe and Draw* using drawings, such as those in Figure 6, which echoed those in the unit.

Games like this started as part of ordinary lessons, but it seemed a pity to use the materials only once, so we started to put drawings on to cards and store them in boxes to be used again.

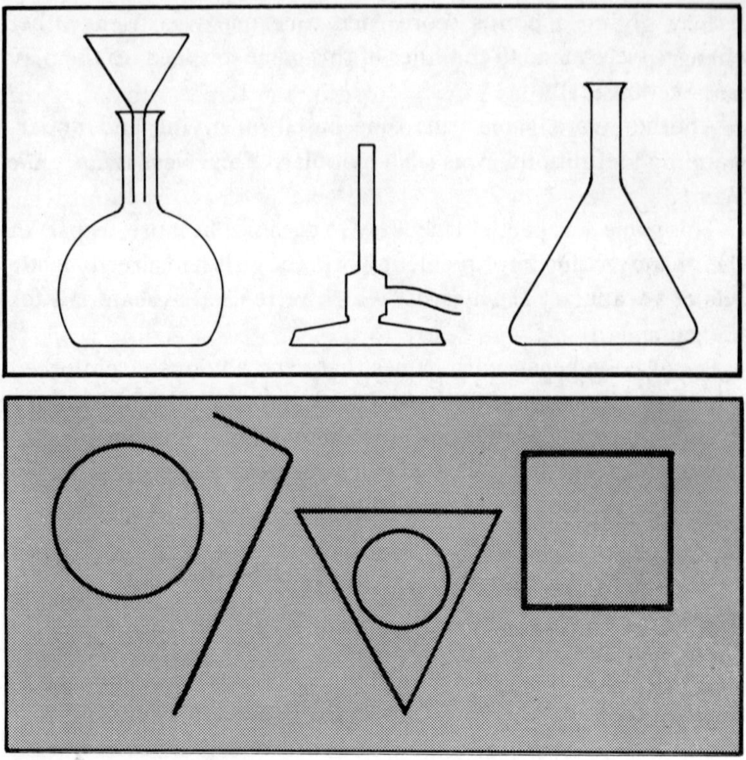

Figure 6 Drawings used in Describe and Draw for science students

A set of ten *Describe and Draw* cards was the basic minimum for a class of twenty girls, and by exchanging cards and partners they would have the chance to try most of them on different occasions. The cards were so easily made that, once the students got the idea, they started making their own, which were put into the box for others to use later.

These students also needed to improve their spelling and word-building, for which *Scrabble*, a published game (see page 134), was useful. It was also more enjoyable than the weekly vocabulary and spelling test. Sometimes we added a rule to encourage players to use as many words as possible from their technical vocabulary list by giving a bonus score each time one was used. Other changes were made to the rules of this game to speed up the play (see Section 6.1).

Another word game, this time based on giving and understanding definitions, was also popular. This was *What's the Word?*

This game was particularly easy to organise because, as part of their handwriting improvement work, the girls had already made sets of vocabulary flash cards, which were used as materials for the game.

Because we began with games that very obviously reinforced other teaching we had little difficulty in persuading these very serious-minded students that what they were doing was worthwhile as well as enjoyable, and games played an important role in activating their passive knowledge of both technical and everyday English.

3.3 Adults (lower intermediate to advanced)

Every year groups of senior French civil servants come to England to study the workings of English Civil Service departments that correspond to their own, and they are given a short refresher course in English to help them derive the most from

WHAT'S THE WORD?

LEVEL Intermediate to Advanced

AGE Teenage to Adult

PLAYERS In pairs

TIMING 5 minutes for 10 cards

Oral/Aural

MAIN LANGUAGE Definition and example, circumlocution and paraphrase

Vocabulary as on each card.

DESCRIPTION Players have a pack of 10 cards between them. Each card has one word written on it. Each player in turn picks up a card and looks at the word but does not let the other player see it. He asks a question or gives a definition or example which will give the other player a clue to the word. If the word is guessed correctly the card is taken by the successful player. If a player fails to guess it the card is replaced at the bottom of the pack to be tried again later.

MATERIALS Small cards, one word written on each card (These should be verbs, nouns, adjectives or adverbs, not grammatical words).

their stay. The emphasis is very much on the listening and speaking skills they will need when attending meetings and holding discussions with their opposite numbers in the UK.

These students need to be equipped to use English within a very short time and for an important purpose, so the courses designed for them must make the best use of the time available. Formal remedial teaching with a considerable amount of language laboratory work forms the core of the course, along with intensive practice in listening skills. Communication games are linked with these components to allow the students to re-use the language they have been revising but in a freer and less predictable framework than controlled practice can provide.

Highly sophisticated groups such as this may already be familiar with communication exercises, since they are used in management training in their own language. One example of a game that has come into language teaching from this field is *The LEGO Game*. Games of this type are readily acceptable to this kind of student because their objectives – in this case, precision in giving instructions – can be immediately understood and appreciated.

More inventive games – ones that require players to find links and similarities between seemingly unrelated ideas and objects – can also be useful with these students. Good examples are *Picture Dominoes* and *If*. Apart from allowing the students to use language functions that are applicable to their professional life – justification, agreement and disagreement, for example – games like this give great scope for imaginative use of language. Irony and sarcasm often emerge in the discussion and this again appeals to more sophisticated students and adds to the general enjoyment. So, although at first sight games like *Picture Dominoes* might seem rather frivolous for adult students, in a course whose purposes are well-defined they offer a welcome opportunity to use language to persuade and amuse as well as to inform one's fellow players.

THE LEGO GAME

LEVEL Intermediate to Advanced   Oral/Aural

AGE Teenage to Adult

PLAYERS In pairs

TIMING 5 minutes to 15 minutes to complete each model

MAIN LANGUAGE Giving instructions, language of position, colours, shapes.

DESCRIPTION Player A has the instruction diagram for how to build a LEGO model. He must not show this to Player B. Player B has the pieces necessary to build the model. Player A describes how the model should be put together. Player B may ask questions if he wishes. When Player B has completed his model he may compare it with the diagram.

MATERIALS LEGO sets or similar children's building materials, and step by step diagrams showing how to build various models.

3.4 One student (any level)

The final case is a situation familiar to many teachers in private language schools and to teachers of students in their own homes – volunteer teachers of immigrants, for example. This is the one-to-one or private lesson, when the only interaction possible is that between the teacher and his one student. Keeping a lesson like this going with sufficient variety of activity and without letting it degenerate into a monologue from the teacher (or the student) can be a problem.

Communication games for pairs can be invaluable, with teacher and student exchanging roles in the game so that each has a turn on each side. Many communication games can be used by advanced players or by beginners. For example, *Find the Difference* can be played by native speakers, even, or by beginners using simple structures such as 'There is a . . . in my picture', 'Can you see a . . . in your picture?' and 'My picture has . . . in it'. Of course the pictures used will have to be chosen so that the vocabulary is within the student's range.

An example of how a communication game can be used with a single student comes from an intensive language improvement course for adults among whom there proved to be one near-beginner. He was taken out of the main classes for some of the time and given intensive tuition in an attempt to bring him to a point where he could hold his own with the main group. He was a highly motivated student, prepared to study at home in an attempt to catch up with the others. The aim was to convert the results of this study into as great a degree of oral fluency and listening ability as was possible in a short time. The strategy adopted was to follow almost every introduction and study of new language with an appropriate communication game, often devised on the spot using visual aids that had been used in the previous part of the lesson. Introducing an information gap which can be crossed by use of language just learned lies behind the transition from class exercise to simple communication game. For example, after learning prepositions both by himself and from class demonstration and discussion with the teacher, the student played *Furnish the Room*.

The student's task was at first mainly to listen and understand, because he was put into the role of the furniture arranger. He was, however, encouraged to ask questions to elicit the information he needed to complete the picture, such as 'Where is the bed?' and 'Is it near the table?'. When all the furniture had been put in place the two pictures could be compared, and the student had practical proof of how well he had understood: if most of the objects had been put in the right parts of the room he knew that he had been successful. Once this stage was over and any misunderstandings had been cleared up, the student was ready to put the new language to active use, so he now took over the role of describer while the teacher tried to follow his instructions and arrange the objects. Again the student had the confidence-boosting evidence that the English he had used was good enough, because it produced the action he wanted from his partner.

3.5 The factors to consider

These four cases illustrate some of the choices that a teacher might make about what games to use with particular students. They also reflect my belief that games are more widely usable and useful than many teachers at first think. What principles can be drawn from these cases? Age, language level, interests and educational background all affect what one can hope to achieve through the use of language games.

Students' ages obviously affect the type of games they can be expected to accept. This is really a matter of commonsense: one would not ask senior government officers to join in a brisk game of *What's the Time, Mr Wolf?*, for example, or expect very

FURNISH THE ROOM

LEVEL Beginners

AGE Children to Adults

PLAYERS pairs
two small teams
a group giving one player instructions

TIMING 2-3 minutes

Oral/Aural

MAIN LANGUAGE
Prepositions
Wh – questions

VOCABULARY
furniture and everyday objects

DESCRIPTIONS Both sides have identical outline pictures of an empty room. Side A has objects and furniture already in place on the picture. Side B has the same objects and furniture separate from the picture. A and B may not look at A's picture. B can ask questions and A give information. The 2 sides cooperate so that B can arrange the furniture and objects in exactly the same way as on A's picture. When all the things are on Picture B, the two sides can compare their pictures and see how closely they resemble each other.

OPTIONS A can watch B and correct any mistakes in placing the pictures or Neither A or B should see the other's picture.

MATERIALS 2 identical outline pictures of an empty room. 2 sets of identical cut out furniture and objects.

young children to be able to cope with making the more abstruse conceptual links demanded by some versions of *If* or *Picture Dominoes.* Teenagers may be the most difficult group to use games with. It might be wise to avoid the word 'game' with them as far as possible and use the word 'activity', so that they do not feel insulted by being treated like children. Adults, on the other hand, often accept a surprising amount of fun provided that it is not artificially and tactlessly imposed on them by some over-enthusiastic games-user. It is important to be sensitive to the mood of the class and to follow it in deciding whether to continue or cut off an activity.

Self-reliance does not necessarily come with age, but it is to be expected on the whole that adults and teenagers will be better at evaluating their own success than will very young children. This is a factor also influenced by education and experience. Many students are reluctant to recognise their own success unless it is endorsed by praise from the teacher; increased monitoring and starting with games in which something is written down or drawn, so that there is a record of an achievement, can start to wean students from this attitude, or of course with some groups it may be better to concentrate on games where the teacher is the judge and awards credit for correct answers or use of language.

Students' attitudes to what a teacher should be doing in the classroom can be deeply entrenched, and he will defy them at his peril. However, there is a difference between gradually altering attitudes by activities that are seen to have some purpose and effect, even though they may seem unusual, and a tactless introduction of new ways of teaching without sufficient explanation or consultation. I have mentioned earlier how students who expected a teacher to be a serious person of some authority were for that very reason prepared to accept my judgement that communication games might be helpful to them.

General sophistication and knowledge of the world are important considerations when deciding whether some games will be suitable for your group. Willingness to experiment with language or to bring one's own experiences into the classroom will also vary, from personality to personality as well as from nationality to nationality. Some games demand a common background culture for them to be successful. One example of this is the well-known English parlour game *Botticelli,* which has the advantage that it can be played with a very limited amount of language. On the other hand, players need a vast amount of shared knowledge.

The next game, *If He Were a Flower,* also uses a limited amount of language in what can be a fascinating way, but to be really successful it needs to be played by students who know each other very well or who have a common circle of friends. It is possible to be very catty or very perspicacious during this game, and it is perhaps best not to introduce it to a group where social relationships are not entirely relaxed – amongst senior and junior colleagues, for example! The structure repeated again and again in this game is the second conditional, but all the attention is on the nouns used to complete each sentence.

I hope there is enough in this book to show that games can be used at any stage in a learner's career and that language level is not a major constraint. One can do complicated things in simple language or simple things in complex language, and games can be found which allow students to do either of these things or anything in between. The only games which might be considered strongly linked to a particular stage in a course are those code-control games that practise a single structure and may cease to be useful once that structure has been mastered. The other types of game – the communication game and the little-and-often skill-based games involving things like spelling, vocabulary-building and pronunciation – can be used again and again throughout a student's career.

It is the teacher's responsibility to choose the activities and adjust his organisation of them in order not only to cater for the

BOTTICELLI

LEVEL Beginners to Advanced (but players must share a common culture in literary and historical terms)

Oral/Aural

AGE Teenage to Adult

PLAYERS Challenger + group

TIMING 3 or 4 minutes per turn

LOCATION Classroom

MAIN LANGUAGE
Are you a .....?
No, I'm not .....

DESCRIPTION The challenger thinks of a famous person or work of art, literature etc., and tells the group the initial letter of his/its name, eg "P" Players try to guess who or what it is by thinking of possible answers which begin with the same initial and asking questions like:

"Are you a famous abstract painter?"

The challenger must guess who it is and answer

eg. "No, I'm not Picasso."

If he cannot supply a name to answer the question this gives the group the right to ask a direct question about the person or thing the challenger is pretending to be.

eg. "Are you a famous city destroyed 2,000 years ago?" (Answer - Pompeii). The challenger fails to answer "No, I'm not Pompeii" so the group may ask eg. "What century do you belong in?" The first player to guess who or what the challenger is takes the place of the challenger.

MATERIALS: None

students' present needs, abilities and expectations, but also to lead them gradually into more adventurous linguistic and conceptual fields.

IF HE WERE A FLOWER

LEVEL Intermediate to Advanced — Oral/Aural

AGE Teenage to Adult

PLAYERS Challenger + group

DURATION 3–4 minutes per turn

LOCATION Classroom

MAIN LANGUAGE

Q If she/he were a ......, what type of ..... would she/he be?

A She/he would be a .....

+extending vocabulary

DESCRIPTION The challenger thinks of a person known to the whole group. The group try to guess who it is by asking "impressionistic" questions like "If he were a flower what type of flower would he be?" The challenger must give an answer that reveals his impression of the person. eg. "He'd be a lily" (for someone rather droopy) or "He'd be a marigold" (for someone rather brash). Other questions could be, "If he were a drink, what would he be?" Answer: "champagne / cold water / hot soup"! etc. The first person to guess who it is changes place with the challenger. N.B. Beware! discussion can become quite violent after the identities are revealed.

MATERIALS: None

4 Making games work in class

Chapter 3 concentrated on using games successfully with different types of student. This chapter looks at how the teacher can organise and direct what students actually do while playing the games.

4.1 Some practical problems

Very often conditions in which people have to teach present problems rather than potential. The first part of this chapter looks at a few obstacles and suggests ways of getting round them, at least partially.

LARGE CLASSES

One of the most often heard reasons for saying 'Games may be all very well, but not with *my* class' is the sheer number of students a teacher may have to deal with at one time. Providing materials for pair games in a class of fifty is obviously beyond a hard-pressed teacher's capacity. Doing teacher-controlled team games may seem to be the answer, but it may be unproductive because of the very limited opportunity each student will get to take part. Are there any games that can be used successfully with very large classes?

One type of game that works well in these circumstances is that in which the answers are not given by individuals from each team but by a whole team at once. These games need not be impossibly noisy since there are many in which players do not have to say anything but can respond silently or signal their choice between two possible answers. *Ship or Sheep?,* for example, can be played with the students putting up their hands if they hear the /ɪ/ sound and putting their heads on their desks if they hear the/i/ sound. Everyone in each team must react at the same time, and there must be no changing of minds. The majority decision is the one that the teacher counts as right or wrong. 50/50 split votes gain no points at all!

Another way of making sure of full participation in a very large class is to base games on the *Bingo* idea.

In its original version *Bingo* is a game of pure chance, with a slight advantage going to people who are attentive listeners to a rapid stream of sound. When adapting it to use for language teaching one can increase the amount of skill needed, but the luck element remains to give the game interest. The numbers can include cardinals, ordinals, fractions, decimals and so on, or there can be pictures on the cards, with the caller giving out the names for the pictures, in which case the game is *Vocabulary Bingo*. Figure 7 gives examples of cards for these two versions. If the pictures are of objects that have similar-sounding names distinguished only by a minimal difference in sound *Pronunciation* or *Minimal Pair Bingo* (published as Sounds Right! – see page 132) can be played. Other types of *Bingo* could require players to make transformations on the language that they hear: *Opposites Bingo,* for example, in which when a player heard a word such as 'good' he would look on his card to see if he had something like 'bad'. *Verb Bingo* (see page 132) is a game in which the players practise linking present stems with irregular past forms. If they hear 'speak', for example, they look for 'spoke' on their cards.

Bingo-type games can solve some of the problems presented by large classes, although of course they can be used with smaller classes too. The materials need not be too hard to make and *Bingo* cards can be used again and again.

BINGO

LEVEL Beginners to Intermediate

AGE Children to Adult

PLAYERS One caller and any number of Bingo players

TIMING 5 minutes upwards - depending on number of cards in the caller's set.

Aural (some versions require players to make grammatical or other transformations)

MAIN LANGUAGE Depends on the content of caller's cards - (See options)

DESCRIPTION The players each have a card ruled into a number of sections. (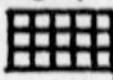) Each section contains a word, a number, or a picture, depending on the version played. Each player's card is different from those of the others.

The caller calls out words or numbers that appear on the cards, each one once only.

If a player has that number or word on his card, he covers it. The first player to cover all of his card shouts 'Bingo!' and is the winner.

OPTIONS Contents of cards can be vocabulary, forms of verbs, numbers, words chosen to practise sound discrimination, etc.

MATERIALS Sets of Bingo cards for each version + list of items for caller, or items written on small cards, which caller picks up + reads at random.

Another type of game that can be used with very large classes is the general contest in which students spend most of the time working quietly by themselves or in small groups before comparing their results and finding out who has done the best. Games like *How Many Words Can You Make?* are suitable for such use.

Vocabulary Bingo

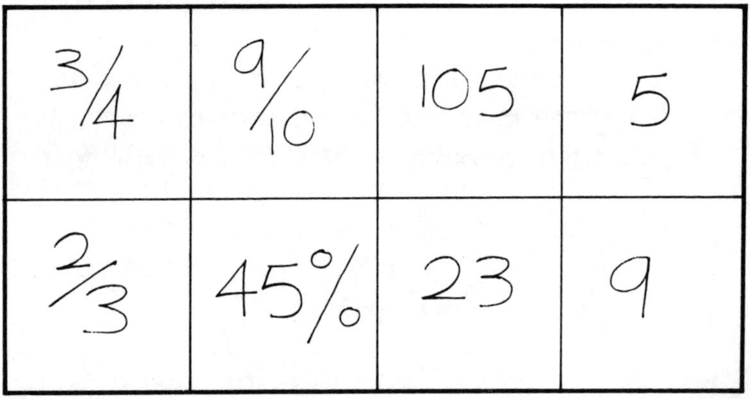

Number Recognition Bingo

Figure 7 Bingo cards

A final possibility for large classes is to have students playing by themselves in small groups but playing games that do not need materials prepared by the teacher. *I Spy, What's My Line?, Hangman,* and *Botticelli* can all be played in this way while the teacher circulates and monitors what is going on.

TOO MUCH NOISE

Of course no one wants a class playing games that disrupt what is going on in the rooms on either side, but this is something that applies to other aspects of teaching too. Students must be trained to play at a necessary rather than a deafening volume, though it is something of a compliment if they get excited enough to want to make a noise! If the feeling in the school against noise is extreme, if there is only a thin partition between one class and the next, or if it is so hot that the windows have to be kept open, there are always the silent 'mass-response' games mentioned above, pencil-and-paper games, and the *Bingo* games, which should not make any more noise than the caller is responsible for.

4.2 Organising games

EXPLAINING WHAT TO DO

Whatever the type of game, the session has to be organised. This means setting up the required groups of students, seeing that they have all the material they need, and above all making sure that they all understand what to do. It is not enough simply to read out the rules of a new game, or to hand out a written copy of the rules. Each game will need a proper introduction, which means an explanation – not just a reading – of the rules, and a short demonstration of a few moves or rounds. You should use the native language at this stage if necessary. It is a waste of time to throw students unprepared into an activity that they have not yet fully grasped: things will go wrong very quickly, and you will then have to spend more time trying to repair the situation. Another reason for giving a full demonstration and explanation of a new game is to show the students exactly what language they can practise as they play it. It is not enough just to say, for example, 'This game is to help you hear the difference between the /ɪ/ sound and the /i/ sound' or 'This game is for practising prepositions'. You need to demonstrate a short part of the game in which you actually make use of the language or the skill that the game is designed to practise. You can then gradually get students joining in. Try to make your demonstration as lively and appealing as possible so that students want to play the game.

SUMMARISING AND COMMENTING

Whatever the game is, students like to hear how well they are doing, to receive encouragement and to have any amusing incidents or clever moves commented on, as well as having errors corrected. This is slightly different from formal feedback on use of language and serves a more social function – to keep a relaxed atmosphere, to show the students that you are interested in what they are doing and to encourage them to be interested in the progress of other players. It is important not to ridicule any individual, of course. Positive comments can be made about individuals but negative comments should be kept more general. Your aim should be to share what people did well with the rest of the class so that everyone can learn from the experience, or to invite suggestions for solving problems from the whole class. The main point of all this is to show the students that what they do with language is interesting. Language can be used cleverly and economically by non-native speakers as well as by native speakers, and games provide a good opportunity for this to be appreciated.

Organising and commenting are things that the teacher needs to do in connection with all games, but otherwise the teacher's role depends very much on the type of game that is being played.

You have to act rather differently during code-control games, where points are generally given for correctness, from the way you act during communication games, where getting the message over is the important thing. The fundamental difference is, of course, that in code-control games the teacher is the only reliable judge of what is correct and thus needs to supervise what goes on, whereas in communication games the students themselves have various means of judging their own success, and the teacher's role is less prominent.

4.3 The teacher's role in code-control games

MASTER OF CEREMONIES/QUIZMASTER

In many of these games it is the teacher who poses the question or challenges the class. It is important to keep up a quick pace and a confident delivery to keep the students on their toes. Hesitation, or a vague searching for what to say next, can make even the best game lose its impetus and seem tedious, so it is a good idea to have some prompts in front of you. For some games, you could have notes or a list of words on a piece of paper, but another way, which ensures that questions do not follow some unconscious repetitive pattern, would be to prepare some one- or two-word prompts on small cards which you can then shuffle and read out as they come. The cards can be useful later as flash cards if you wish to reinforce and draw attention to any of the points in the game when you are summarising and commenting on it.

Some games like *What's My Line?* have a fairly long interval between challenges because players have to ask several questions before they arrive at the solution to the puzzle, but it is still useful to have a collection of prompt cards, since they will be helpful if you wish to hand over the role of challenger to one of the class. If a student takes one of the cards and uses the idea or the word on it, he cannot cheat by changing his mind about what the correct answer is in the middle of his turn!

JUDGE/EVALUATOR OF RESPONSES

If marks are awarded in a game for correct use of language there must be someone to judge correctness. Usually the only person able to do this is the teacher. Even in games in which students can take over the role of quizmaster or challenger, the teacher will have the last word on what language is acceptable. Decisions should be absolutely clear and firm and made without irritation at those students who continually get things wrong. You should make a mental note about future remedial work that is needed rather than hold up the game and start teaching in the middle of it. Further explanations and remedial work can be given afterwards. Students who fail to get an answer right will very often of their own accord listen more carefully to their fellow players in an effort to find out for themselves where they went wrong, so that they can do better on their next turn.

You need some clear and, if possible, dramatic way of indicating approval or rejection of an answer. Silently putting another mark on the scoreboard is not the most exciting way of accepting an answer. Children often enjoy some pantomine from the teacher – a thumbs-down sign, for example, an exaggerated grimace, or perhaps even a small bell for the right answers and a hooter for grotesquely wrong ones would all make it absolutely clear whether an answer is being accepted or rejected. You could hesitate dramatically sometimes to keep the students alert and to elicit their opinions on whether an answer is right or wrong. There is a serious point to all this: quick effective feedback on correctness is essential if students are to learn both from their mistakes and from their right answers, especially in those games that are really extensions of language drills. Combining fun and good teaching practice is the essence of successful games sessions.

SCORER

Winning a point for a right answer is a powerful motivator, particularly with younger classes. It does not have to be the teacher who makes the marks on the scoreboard. This is a task that some students love, and it need not prevent them from taking part in the game as well. There are many ways of recording scores (see Figure 8), some of which are instructive in themselves. The teacher needs a good range of these so that he can vary the method from game to game. The students might even invent some new ways of scoring that you could add to your list. They should look as interesting as possible but not be too complicated. It should be possible to tell the relative positions of the players or teams at a glance.

Building up a picture is a popular way of scoring. The best-known example is in the spelling game *Hangman,* in which every wrong guess allows the challenger to draw another line of the scaffold and hanged man. You could also build up a picture by counting the *right* answers. In this case, the teams could compete to see whose picture will be completed first. You could build up a picture of an insect or a spider, for example, adding bits of its body and each leg one by one. You should choose things that are easily split up into quickly drawn parts so that scoring does not hold the game up.

Another possibility is to show rival stick men climbing up something step by step until they reach the top – going up a ladder rung by rung, for example, or climbing a mountain. Because a stick man or other figure takes some time to draw, this method of scoring is probably better for games like *What's in the Bag?,* in which the scores do not come as thick and fast as they do in the more quick-fire yes/no type of game such as *Ship or Sheep?*

Other ways of scoring can teach something in themselves. For example, each team could be competing to finish the alphabet from A to Z, one letter being added every time a team scores a point. Alternatively each team could be racing to finish a long word letter by letter or they could be progressing through the days of the week or the months of the year.

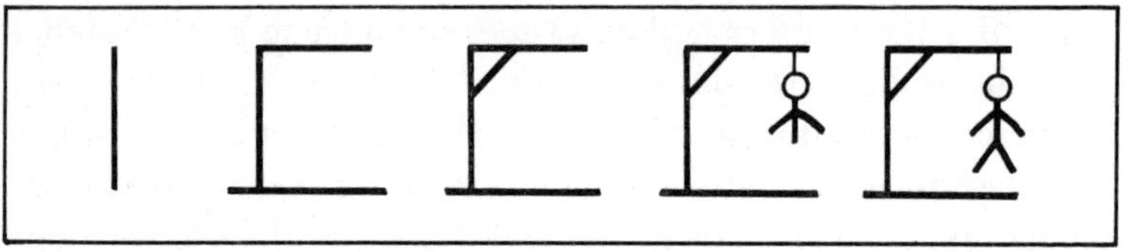

Hangman (built up one line at a time)

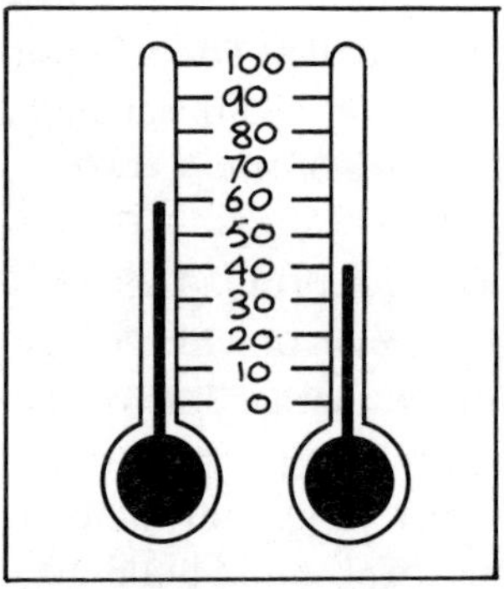

Rival thermometers—each side moves up 10° at a time

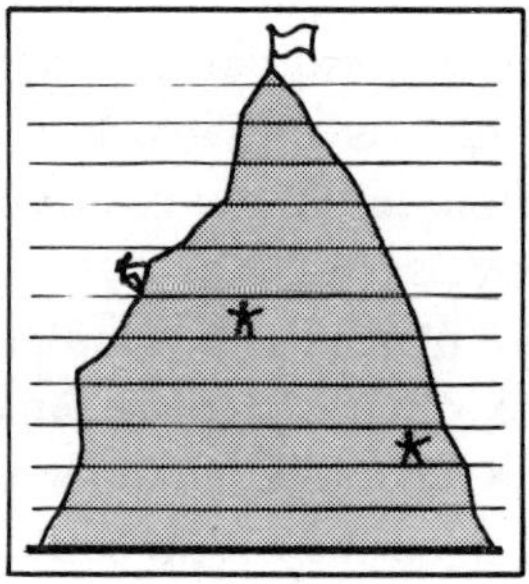

Climbing a mountain

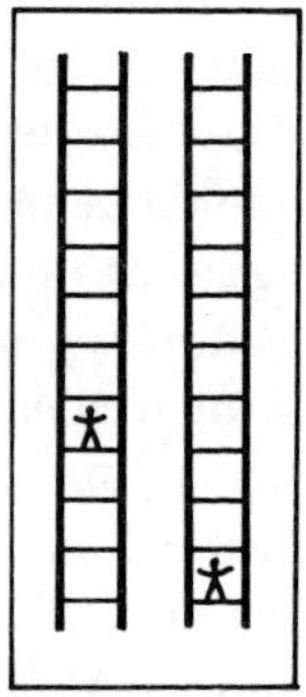

Climbing ladders

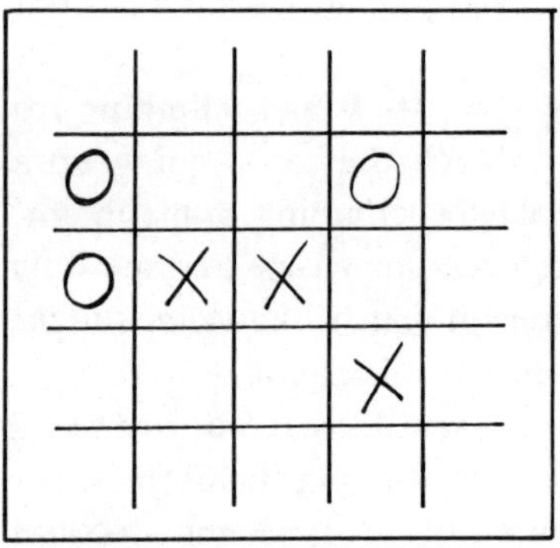

Noughts and Crosses (a game within a game)—the aim is to get five of one's symbols in a row

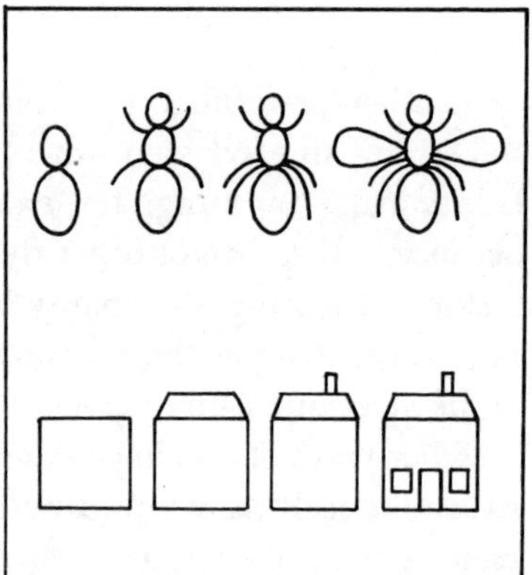

Other simple built-up pictures

Figure 8 Ways of scoring

Scoring can also provide a game within a game. A sketch of a football pitch can be drawn on the board, and the number of stages between the centre line and the goal agreed. For every point that each team wins, the ball moves one stage nearer to their opponents' goal. When it reaches a goal the 'football' game could end there, or the ball could be returned to the centre line and the process started again. Another idea would be to have a giant game of noughts and crosses played on the board, the aim being for one team to put five noughts or five crosses in a straight line before the other team can complete its lines. This would encourage each team to try to get as many correct answers in a row as possible, so as to prevent the other team putting in a nought or a cross to block one of their lines. This type of scoring involves a tactical decision about the best place to put one's mark. Two scorers could be appointed, one from each team, to be responsible for the tactics. In a more leisurely game they could take instructions from their teams about where to put the marks. This allows students to practise language like 'the top left hand corner' or 'the middle square'.

4.4 The teacher's role in communication games

In communication games the teacher no longer controls the activity. In fact he would be distorting their whole purpose if he interfered too much. The interaction should be between student and student rather than students and teacher.

INFORMANT/LANGUAGE CONSULTANT

Instead of judging what students have to say, the teacher should now be on hand to help them with what they want to say. Students should know that you are there to be used as a source of information – perhaps on vocabulary or on new structures, or with a suggestion about how they could rephrase something to make it clearer to other players. It is usually better for the teacher to wait until he is asked for help than to jump in and take over the game when players are struggling. Part of the training consists in the struggling and experimenting with the language to try to get the message across. When you are asked for help you should stop to think whether the students really need new linguistic information or whether you can lead them towards expressing themselves in language they already know. If so, you should try to elicit this language from them rather than simply supplying it. The aim should always be to show students that they can manage in more situations than they think they can.

MONITOR/CORRECTOR

Although the teacher does not act as a judge during communication games there is plenty of scope for observing students' performances and doing something about serious errors or areas of ignorance. In these games the range of language used is as wide or as limited as the students can manage. The players are often very intensely involved in the task they are trying to complete and this may cause them to experiment with language and go beyond what they know how to say. This may lead to errors, but error is an essential part of the experimentation. Provided that the errors are not so serious that they lead to breakdowns in communication, the other players may not notice them (although players do often correct each other).

In terms of the game the errors do not matter, but how is the teacher to deal with them? If you stop a game completely and start teaching or revising a language point, the whole atmosphere will be spoiled; students may even get the idea that the games have only been set to trap them into mistakes, and if this happens, they may become too self-conscious to get anything very much out of the activities. There is no harm, however, in making quick corrections of some of the errors that you hear as you go from group to group. You should go for major points rather than for mere slips of the tongue, and for points that do not require a lengthy explanation, such as incorrect question-forms. For some reason these forms often go seriously wrong in the excitement of a game. Correction should be as indirect as possible – just a look at the offender as a signal that something is wrong often elicits the correct form, for example. You should use your judgement about whether intervening will disrupt the game too much, and if there is a danger of this, don't do it!

But what about more serious problems? Some errors or gaps in knowledge may need several minutes of explanation. You should collect information on these things as you go round, with a view to incorporating them in your lessons later on. Some teachers simply make a mental note, but others prefer to record the information more systematically. It is a good idea to carry a small notepad with you as you monitor. The essential things to write down are what the errors are and who is making them. In other words you need to be able to distinguish the difficulties that individuals are having from those that are common to the whole group, since it would obviously be a waste of time to re-teach the whole class something that only one or two students needed help with. The common difficulties are likely to be those you know only too well. However, communication games can also be very valuable in revealing difficulties you never suspected, whether in language or in skills. You may find that one student is unexpectedly weak in his use of tenses, or that another is incapable of listening to the detail of what his partner is saying – things which might not emerge so clearly in the course of a normal lesson.

If you wish to keep a systematic record, it is worthwhile putting headings on your notepad rather than just jotting down notes on a scribbled piece of paper. This monitoring sheet need not be at all elaborate – just a few columns ruled giving general headings under which to group the errors, with one column left to write in the students' names or an indication that the error is one of general relevance. A suggested layout for such a sheet appears in Figure 9. If you want to keep your monitoring sheets for future reference you will also need to write in the class name and the date. It is a good idea also to write down the names of the games from which you get the information. Your monitoring sheet will then serve another purpose, as well as being a record of deficiencies, because you can collect useful information about

Game Gifts for the Family		Class Date	
Student	Lexis error correct	Syntax	Pronunciation error correct
Pierre	sensible sensitive	You will give her a thing so cheap	suːtəbl sjuːtəbl
Claude		I no like that	
Language occurring frequently			

Figure 9 Game monitoring sheet

the type of language that each game does in fact elicit. You may realise when looking through your monitoring sheet that a particular game could be used for a language point that you had never connected with it before. This information will also be useful to your colleagues, so you should make sure that you add a note to the description of the game on the catalogue sheet, as recommended in Chapter 8. For further advice on analysis and treatment of students' errors, consult *Language Learners and their Errors* by John Norrish in this series.

ARBITER/REFEREE

Some communication games are competitive, and there may well be disagreements and blockages that the group cannot settle on its own. The links some players make between picture cards in a game like *Picture Dominoes* can be too far-fetched for their opponents to accept and you may be called in to arbitrate. It is much more effective to try to guide the group towards its own solution than to impose an immediate decision of your own since by this means you can get valuable discussion going within the group. To try to settle a dispute, you can set players to read the rules of the game again. This is very good practice in reading for detail. You can require a player to justify his move to you before you give your casting vote. Do not spend too long acting as arbiter, however: your prime concern should be to get the players going again without you.

Another sort of intervention you may have to make is more like refereeing than arbitration. While students are still getting used to the idea of communication games, and before they have fully grasped the point of the exercise, you may find that in their excitement, or their frustration at not being able to get their exact message over in a foreign language, they slip into their native tongue. In a way it is a compliment to the game that they are so determined to play it successfully, but it does thwart the opportunity for language practice that you are trying to give them! The way to deal with this sort of 'cheating' is not through dire threats but by increasing the amount of help and advice you give at this stage. Make sure that the students realise that the challenge is not so much to succeed in the game itself, but to succeed by using the foreign language. This is one of the rules of the game, if you like.

There is no reason why, if the students enjoy a game for itself, they should not play it at other times in their own language. (Make sure, however, that this happens outside your lessons!) They may even transfer the strategies that they use to play it in their native language into the foreign language, and this could be very valuable. Communication games are, after all, not specific to any one language: they just require language. Although the suggestions in this chapter concern games, most of what underlies them is common to most successful teaching – preparing the lesson and, if necessary, organising the classroom beforehand, having confidence in the materials and using them with definite objectives in mind, making sure that the students know what you want to achieve so that they have confidence in you and the materials, being supportive rather than punitive, eliciting what people know before you supply them with what they do not know, and above all trying to develop strategies that will be useful for later learning.

5 When to use games

Language games are often used to fill in a few minutes at the end of a lesson, or to occupy some of the faster students while the others catch up on an exercise. There is nothing wrong in this, but this chapter is mainly about integrating games much more closely into lessons and into the teaching syllabus so that they become one of the means of achieving teaching objectives rather than just an enjoyable 'extra'. Figure 10 summarises some of the uses to which games can be put.

5.1 Teaching new language

This section draws on a simple and widely accepted view of what should happen during most lessons in which a new piece of language is being taught. There are three main stages in the process of bringing students from a state in which the new language is completely unknown to them to the ability to start using it confidently by themselves. These stages are (a) presentation of the new language item, (b) giving the students controlled practice in its use, and (c) giving them the chance to use the language in a situation in which they have to communicate. The teacher's aim and the techniques he can use at each stage are outlined in Figure 10, but the overall purpose is concerned with what will happen outside the classroom. The aim is to equip students with a grasp of language that will serve them in real life.

When using a game as part of a lesson, it is important to make sure that the way in which it is played – the interaction among

Stage in teaching	Teacher's aim	Teacher's and students' roles	Types of game
Presentation	Provide a good model of the new language Make its meaning clear Check students' understanding	Teacher is the centre of attention Students respond to teacher's cues to show their understanding	Played by whole class under teacher's direction Competitive Teacher is judge of responses and scorer Responses are simple actions or yes/no answers; players do not yet produce new language themselves eg O'Grady Says
Controlled practice (drills and exercises)	Elicit a good imitation of the model from students Elicit new language as an appropriate response to a situation or context Help students perform grammatical transformations on the new language	Teacher cues and directs what the class does, but the interactions are more varied, eg teacher–class, teacher–individual, individual–individual, group–group Teacher corrects as necessary	Played by whole class under teacher's direction Competitive Teacher is judge of responses and scorer Players must produce the language correctly and appropriately and/or do correct transformations on it eg Who Is It?
Communicative practice	Give opportunities to use the language to affect other people's actions, eg give instructions, persuade, solve a problem	Teacher steps out of the limelight Students interact directly as, eg, pairs, small groups, or as individual and small group Teacher monitors groups and advises players when needed	Individual, pair or small-group games not under direct control of teacher Players must use language to achieve practical aim Cooperative or competitive Students can judge their own success eg Describe and Draw, Find Your Partner

Figure 10 Types of game suitable at the three stages of teaching new language

the players and the role the teacher plays in it – fits with the stage in the lesson that has been reached. During the presentation stage, for example, it is normal for all the students' attention to be on the teacher as they try to assimilate both the meaning and the form of the new language item. It would therefore not be good teaching practice to use a game at this stage in which the students have to talk in pairs. Not only would their grasp of the new language not be well enough established for them to use it independently, but the pair arrangement would conflict with the teacher/class pattern of interaction which is the most appropriate to this part of a lesson. On the other hand, a game in which the teacher acts as master of ceremonies and as judge with the students competing under his control would fit this stage much better. However, in the final stage of a lesson when the students are ready to use the newly learned language in a freer and more flexible way it would be a waste of opportunity to tie them down to a game controlled by the teacher. Students would have more time to talk and would be talking to more purpose if they were given a game to be played in pairs or small groups with the teacher no longer the controller or judge but more of an adviser and language informant.

Chapter 1 considered some of the features of games that can be varied – such things as the number of players, the way in which they are grouped, and whether they are competing or cooperating. The point of varying a game in this way is not just to provide a nice change but to make sure that the game you want to play to practise a particular language point involves interaction appropriate to the type of practice you are trying to set up.

It is not being suggested that a game be used at *each* stage of any one lesson, but as a practical illustration of how the same language item could form the basis of games at the presentation stage, the controlled practice stage and the communicative practice stage, let us take a simple structure that occurs early in most courses: *a/the man with a/the big nose.*

PRESENTATION

Let us suppose that you have started to introduce this structure by commenting on magazine pictures or your own line drawings, for example, showing people with distinctive features like blue eyes, red hair or big ears. What you should do at this stage is provide a good model of the language for the students to imitate and help them understand its meaning and use. To do these things you need to repeat the language many times in unambiguous contexts that make its meaning unmistakable.

The following game, *Which One Is It?*, could be used to vary the activity and provide a change of pace while at the same time giving a good reason to repeat the language. The students have to react to what they hear, so they are actively involved even at this stage of the lesson.

The game illustrates a typical and authentic use of the structure, namely as a means of distinguishing one object or person from a number of similar ones. The students have to pick out one picture from several according to a description which the teacher gives. In the version to be used in the presentation stage the teacher puts up about twelve large drawings of faces. There should be roughly equal numbers of male and female faces. Each face is similar in outline to the others but varies in details such as the size of ears or nose, the length of hair or the colour of eyes or hair. Each face has some simple means of identifying it written beside it: a letter, a number or, more amusingly, a short, easily read name. The pictures could be ready-drawn on a large piece of card, or sketched on the blackboard before the lesson starts and hidden until needed. Alternatively, some of the pictures already used to introduce the language could be fixed on the blackboard – the most time-saving and flexible method. The result might look something like Figure 11.

The class is split into two equal teams. Students must answer in turn within each team, but for every turn, two students, one from each team, are competing to see who can answer first. The teacher

WHICH ONE IS IT?

LEVEL Beginners — Oral / Aural

AGE Children to Adults

PLAYERS Challenger + whole class
Challenger + competing teams
Challenger + small group

TIMING 5–10 minutes

LOCATION Classroom

MAIN LANGUAGE

A The	man	with	a the	...

DESCRIPTION About 12 pictures differing in a few details are put up in front of the class. Each picture can be identified by a name or a number. The challenger describes one of the pictures without pointing to it.

eg. "the woman with the big nose."

Players compete to see who can identify the picture referred to.

OPTIONS This can be played in teams with players answering in turn or players can compete to give the correct answer first.

MATERIALS Large pictures or photographs of people, animals etc., distinguished by a few prominent characteristics, like big noses, red hair etc.

Figure 11 Drawings for Which One Is It?

describes one of the pictures without pointing to it, eg 'The lady with green eyes'. The first student to call out the correct name wins a point for his team. If he calls out the wrong name, the other team gets a point,and their representative has the chance to try for the correct name, thus having the chance of another point. The teacher could leave it up to the class to challenge any answers they think are incorrect; the chance of catching the other team out would keep everyone alert.

Notice how the fact that this is the presentation stage of the lesson has influenced the way in which the game is organised. It is a team game because the teacher has to keep control of the class responses and to provide instant feedback on correctness at a stage when the students have not yet mastered the new language. He can do this most conveniently by acting as the main speaker and the judge, awarding points in the game as part of the feedback. At this stage the students are not producing the form themselves. They respond and show their understanding of it by calling out the appropriate name.

CONTROLLED PRACTICE

During this stage of the lesson the teacher should give the students the opportunity to start producing the language themselves. Drills are one way of doing this, but the next version of *Which One Is It?* can be used along with drills to vary the activity a little.

Pictures like those in Figure 11 can be used, and the students are again in competing teams. This time one student from each team takes his turn at describing one of the pictures and challenging one of the other team to identify it. The teacher sees fair play and keeps the score as before. To prevent challengers changing their minds about what picture they are describing in the middle of their turn the teacher could give out slips of paper with the name or number of each picture on them or require players to write down which they are describing before they start to talk about it.

The same idea may be used in a more personal way in a game called *Who Is It?*

This need not be played as a team game but as a turn-taking game so that the first person to guess who is being described comes up and takes the place of the challenger. Alternatively the person described could become the challenger. The description might need to be quite lengthy before enough details are given to distinguish one student from another, eg 'It's a boy with fair hair . . . and blue eyes . . . and a red pullover'. As a variation, players may be allowed to ask the challenger questions to help them guess. Again, as a precaution against accusations of cheating, it might be a good idea to have each student whisper to the teacher the name of the person who is being described at the beginning of the turn.

These games fit in with the type of class organisation suitable for the controlled practice stage. The teacher can still check and give feedback on correctness, but now the students are given the chance to use the new structure for themselves.

WHO IS IT?

LEVEL Beginners
AGE Child to Adult
PLAYERS Challenger + whole class
Challenger + competing teams
TIMING 5-10 minutes
LOCATION Classroom

Oral/Aural

MAIN LANGUAGE
"I'm thinking of a boy with..."
"Is it John?"

DESCRIPTION The challenger describes someone in the class, saying eg. "I'm thinking of a girl with fair hair". Class can cross-question. They are competing to see who can be the first to recognise the person described.

OPTIONS The successful guesser can win a point for his team.
The successful guesser can take the challenger's place.
The person described can take the challenger's place.

MATERIALS None.

COMMUNICATIVE PRACTICE

By this stage the students should be producing the new language with confidence and will be ready to try using it more independently of the teacher. There must be some very clear way for each student to check on his own success since the teacher will not be able to listen to everything that is said. The best method of doing this is to have some instant visual means of checking. An example of this appears in the next game.

This version of *Find Your Partner* needs each student to have a card with a simple line drawing on it. Each drawing has an identical counterpart so that for every student there is a 'partner'

Student A I've got a lady with a big hat.'
Student B 'So have I.'

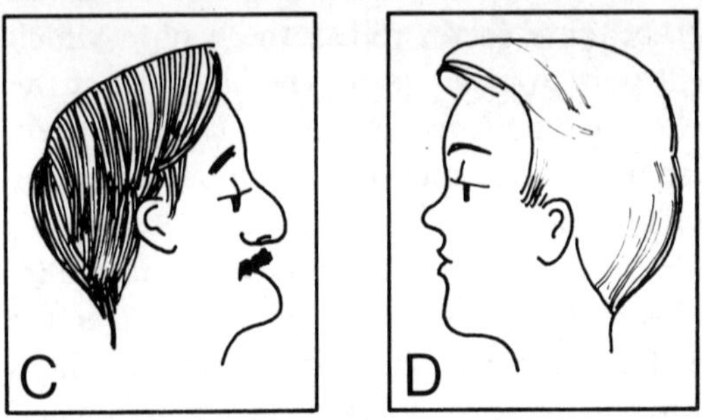

Student C 'Have you got a man with a big nose?'
Student D 'No, I haven't.'

Figure 12 Cards for Find Your Partner

who has the same picture. Photocopies of an original set of pictures are a quick way of providing duplicates. Students must not show each other their cards but must go around asking each other 'What have you got?' or 'Have you got a . . . with a . . .' and describing their own cards. Figure 12 gives some examples of cards.

Another way in which this language can be used as part of a game to give communicative practice is in this version of *Describe and Arrange*. The pictures to be arranged need to be of the same type as those used in the other games so that the 'x with y' structure is naturally elicited. However, this game will obviously call for language other than this structure – for example, prepositional phrases such as 'next to' and 'to the right of'. Various ways of instructing one's partner how to place the picture cards can be used, from the imperative 'Put the dog with the long tail under the dog with the black ears' to the statement which implies an instruction 'There is a cat with a blue face next to a cat with green ears . . . on the right.' This type of game offers a simple framework for experimenting with language even at this early stage in a course.

By adjusting the visual content of the cards for *Find Your Partner* and *Describe and Arrange* the main language focus can be changed, but both of these games reflect the way in which we hope students will start to make use of the language at the communicative stage of teaching. Even at a simple language level they have the satisfaction of seeing their fellows do something or react as a result of what is said.

The teacher's role in these games fits in with the greater independence he wants his students to show. He is no longer the controller and judge of every move or exchange, but circulates among the players on a more equal footing, as a monitor and language informant, helping out with language difficulties and keeping a note of points that will need to be revised or covered in later lessons.

DESCRIBE AND ARRANGE

LEVEL Beginners to Advanced
AGE Children to Adults
PLAYERS Pairs
TIMING 3–5 minutes for each set of pictures
LOCATION Classroom

Oral/Aural
MAIN LANGUAGE
Language of description and location
Instructions

DESCRIPTION Player A has a set of pictures arranged in a pattern. Player B has the same pictures but they are separate. Player B may not see the way A's pictures are arranged. A and B must exchange information so that B can arrange his pictures in the same order as A's. When B has completed the arrangement the two sets of pictures may be compared.

MATERIALS Sets of identical pictures. A's may be glued into place on a piece of card, or he may make his own arrangement (which must be kept hidden from B).

5.2 'Little-and-often' practice

This category covers games that can be used again and again, gradually building up skills by constant practice. The emphasis is on skills rather than language structures or functions. Pronunciation is an area that all students may need help with throughout their language-learning careers but which it is difficult to deal with in isolation in a way that is acceptable to most classes. Games cannot provide the essential information about how to make sounds, but pronunciation and sound-discrimination games can make practice in this area much more lively and entertaining. Counting and spelling games and games which involve recall of vocabulary are also suitable for little-and-often use. Examples from this book are *Hangman, Bingo, Ship or Sheep?* and *How Many Words Can You Make?*

Vocabulary games like *The Minister's Cat* provide a good chance for students to show off their knowledge and learn something from one another, even if in this case the scope for extending one's knowledge of adjectives when the letter x is reached is fairly limited: the minister's cat is nearly always 'xenophobic'! This type of game promotes the use of dictionaries, either during the game (allowable if players do not exceed the time limit for answering) or in the discussion and comments session that naturally develops after the game.

In pencil-and-paper games students can learn from each other's answers as well as develop word-building and writing skills individually.

5.3 Revision

The simplest and most obvious way in which games can be used to help students revise is to play some games again from time to time. A game which is liked and well-known to the class may also

THE MINISTER'S CAT

<u>LEVEL</u> Intermediate to Advanced

<u>AGE</u> Teenage to Adult

<u>PLAYERS</u> Competing against each other. Teacher as Master of ceremonies.

<u>TIMING</u> 5-10 minutes

<u>LOCATION</u> Classroom

Oral/Aural

<u>MAIN LANGUAGE</u> Adjectives Alphabetical order

<u>DESCRIPTION</u> Players take it in turns to say something about the Minister's cat,

"The Minister's cat is an athletic cat"

"The Minister's cat is a beautiful cat"

going through the alphabet with the adjectives inserted in the sentence. Anyone who cannot think of an adjective or who makes a mistake in alphabetical order is eliminated. The last player in is the winner.

<u>MATERIALS</u> None.

act as a useful point of reference. Recalling something that happened in a game may help a student remember the language connected with it. Other games may be quite new to the students but call for language that they have already covered. For example, *Past-Tense Knockout* might be played for the revision of irregular past tenses.

Just by noting how quickly students are eliminated for not knowing an answer the teacher can get a rough idea of how much remedial teaching he will have to do. It is of course important that a game like this should not in any way be seen by the players as a disguised test.

5.4 Diagnosis

With a new class whose language abilities one wants to assess, orally at least, communication games can be very useful. Giving students games like *Describe and Draw* and *Describe and Arrange* to play in pairs is a good way of getting this information quickly. Monitoring what goes on and taking notes on the monitoring sheet suggested in Chapter 4 will produce a record of errors and language areas to deal with in later lessons.

5.5 General fluency

Games should be integrated more closely with mainstream classroom teaching, but they do not belong only in lessons. Communication games, in particular, can be used in their own right as a way of increasing students' fluency and confidence. Students are often free to choose games they would like to try from a selection offered, either on the shelves of a student resources centre, or more simply when the teacher brings a number of different games into class. The language used in a communication game need not be restricted to a few structures, but this can be done with new

PAST TENSE KNOCKOUT

LEVEL Intermediate to Advanced — Oral/Aural
AGE Children to Adult
PLAYERS Teacher + whole class, unsuccessful players eliminated.
TIMING 5 minutes +
LOCATION Classroom

MAIN LANGUAGE Irregular past tenses - in or out of a context.

DESCRIPTION Players stand, in a ring if possible, and the teacher gives each in turn the present stem or past participle or other part of an irregular verb as a stimulus for them to produce the correct past form. Any player who makes a mistake is eliminated and must sit down. The last player left "in" is the winner. When one player makes a mistake or cannot answer the teacher does not give the correct answer but passes to the next player in the ring.

OPTIONS Players can simply be given the present stem and be required to respond, eg. "buy → bought," but it is better to put the verbs into a sentence. Exchanges such as "Have you seen Tom this week?" — "Yes I saw him yesterday." "Have you bought a newspaper this week?" — "Yes I bought one yesterday." or "Are you seeing your friend today?" — "No, I saw him yesterday." can provide a formula for the game. MATERIALS None language. Language functions can be performed at many different levels of linguistic complexity, so that a game which consists essentially of giving one's partner instructions can be played by elementary students or by native speakers. Students enjoy being faced with a game as a challenge – to find out what they can and cannot say in the target language.

The teacher's role as language informant is even more important in these circumstances when students are genuinely eager to fill in gaps in their knowledge that they have discovered for themselves. The fact that these gaps are not revealed in public but rather discovered when students are engrossed in a task and determined to succeed in it is very important for their attitude to this new information and their consequent retention of it. The teacher must be prepared to work extremely hard, though unobtrusively, in these sessions, but other sources of information should be available at the same time: normal learners' dictionaries, of course, for verifying words and meanings, but also simple picture-dictionaries, which are extremely useful for letting students find out about 'missing' bits of vocabulary for themselves.

Some games are functionally based, that is they are designed round a language function such as giving instructions, as in *Describe and Draw,* but many games elicit less predictable and less easily teachable functions. *Gifts for the Family* and *Picture Dominoes,* for example, are based on the justification of arguments but also often give rise to strong disagreement. Sometimes protests and even threats are to be heard as real life interaction comes ever closer in the heat of the moment!

Games that are to be used frequently need to be durably constructed and to have clear instructions attached to each one to supplement the teacher's initial explanation of how to play each one and prevent him having to spend too much time sorting out problems to do with understanding the rules. Suggestions on making games appear in Chapter 7.

6 Adapting and inventing games

Most games can easily be changed to suit your classes in ways suggested in Chapters 1 and 5, but you may still wish to branch out and make something new of your own. The choice is between adaptation of games not intended for the classroom into something that can be used as a teaching aid, and creation from scratch of your own teaching games.

6.1 Adapting games

Not everyone has an immediate flair for inventing games, but a lot can be learnt about what goes into a good game from trying to adapt existing games to one's purposes. The raw material has been widely successful with ordinary people; now the amount of language used during the game must be increased without distorting it beyond recognition – and enjoyment.

INCREASING OPPORTUNITIES FOR TALK

Word games like *Scrabble* and board games like *Monopoly* are commercially available games (see page 134 for details) that are widely enjoyed, but they do not generate enough language as they stand to justify their use as part of a language course. Even though *Scrabble* uses words, it can be a very silent affair, and in *Monopoly* most of the language generated is mere comment on the state of play rather than an integral part of what is going on. Comments like 'Oh dear!' and 'That's bad luck!' may be fun to learn, but they hardly justify playing a game that can take several hours in its original version! In order to get your students talking as a way of keeping the game going you may have to interfere slightly with the original rules or perhaps remove or alter some of the original material.

The first and obvious thing to do is to add a rule to the game saying that each player must open and close his move with a remark, either about what he intends to do or about what he has just done. For example, *Scrabble* can be livened up by building in a rule that a player who makes a new word must also be able to tell the other players its meaning before he can collect his score. It can be an extremely slow game, especially when non-native speakers are puzzling over the words that they could make, but a time limit on each move helps to speed things up, and appointing a time-keeper amongst the group to hurry players along gives another reason for talk during the game.

In a board game like *Monopoly,* players often have to take Chance or Penalty cards and obey the instructions on them. Opportunities for talk can be increased by requiring players to ask for these cards rather than take them silently, and by making it a rule that another player should read the instructions on the card out loud to the group rather than having a player read his own card silently. A listening comprehension element can be added to the game in this way. The Chance cards themselves can be altered or replaced to create more reasons for players to talk to one another. For example, a Chance card in *Monopoly* that says 'You may claim £1000 from any other player' is bound to set up a discussion as each player tries to think of reasons why he should not be the person from whom the money is claimed! Any game that has Chance cards in it can be treated in the same way. The aim should always be to add cards that will cause conflict and discussion amongst the group.

Changing the ways in which the moves are made can also bring about more talk. Many board games use the throw of a die to decide how many spaces a player may move, but this requires little or no talking: an alternative is to have the move decided by the result of a calculation, which of course must be done aloud in the target language. There could be two dice or spinners whose numbers could be added together (see Figure 25 for how to make a spinner). A more complex way would be to have two dice and a spinner whose faces showed plus, minus, multiplication, and division signs. Each player would then throw his two numbers on the dice and would have to combine them with the mathematical signs showing on the spinner. He would then have to work out the sum that was the most advantageous to him. It might, for example, suit him best to move backwards on a particular turn, in which case he could try to combine his numbers to produce a negative number. So, if he threw a 6, a 3 and a minus sign, he could choose to make the sum $3-6=-3$ and move back three spaces. Another possibility would be to have instruction cards with messages on them like 'Go forward 7' or 'Go back 1' written on each one. These cards could be put into a pile and one could be taken at random by each player when his turn came. Either he could read it aloud or another player could pick it up and read it to him, so providing listening practice.

These are all suggestions for ways of making students use language to keep the game going – to mark the transition from move to move or to negotiate with one another during a move. In this way, even the relatively slow word games whose chief value is that they teach students more *about* language – spelling and vocabulary in the case of *Scrabble* – can have some talk and discussion built into them.

CHANGING THE SUBJECT MATTER

Another reason for adapting a well-known game is that its subject matter is not suited or acceptable to all students even though the rules of the game itself would provide players with a good reason for using language. A good example of this is *Happy*

Families: in the original card game players try to collect sets of cards showing members of the same family by asking each other questions and claiming any card that they rightly guess another player to have. Clearly, in a game like this, players will listen very carefully to one another since they are trying to remember who has got each card. This would seem to make *Happy Families* a very suitable game for language learners. The only problem may be that the cards themselves are too childish for older students to wish to use. You could, however, keep the rules unaltered but make your own sets of cards with different subject matter, more suitable to your students' tastes or interests. Each set within a game can consist of more or fewer cards than the four which make up the families in the original. *Mathematical Happy Families* could contain sets of fractions, geometrical figures and mathematical signs, for example. Types of food (three types of meat, three types of tinned food, three fruits, etc) could form the basis of another game. Because the links between objects like this are less obvious than in the original game you will also need to provide a list of what is on all the cards for students to refer to during the game.

Another well-known card game which you could adapt for language learners by changing the materials is *Snap*.

In the traditional game the players alternately put picture cards down one by one in two piles until cards showing the same thing are seen side by side. The first player to shout 'Snap!' can pick up all the cards on the table. For language learners it would obviously be a waste of time to play this game using only picture cards, since there would be no language exercised at all except for the regular cry of 'Snap'. However, using a combination of picture cards with word cards referring to the pictures, the players would have to try to match vocabulary to image and would be competing to read the words on the cards more quickly than their partners. On seeing a matching pair they could call out 'Snap' or say aloud the vocabulary item itself. Another version of

VOCABULARY SNAP

LEVEL Beginners to Intermediate Reading + Oral
AGE Children
PLAYERS In competing pairs
TIMING 5 minutes
LOCATION Classroom
MAIN LANGUAGE Vocabulary

DESCRIPTION A pack of cards is dealt equally between the two players. They take it in turns to place their cards down face upwards in two piles. If two identical cards are showing at any time, the players shout "Snap!"
The first player to do so wins all the cards that have been put down so far. The game ends when all the cards have been won by one player.
MATERIALS Picture and word cards, with several identical cards in the pack.

the same game could involve matching chemical symbols and formulae to the names of chemical substances. Such games would be useful to those students who had to learn the equivalents in English to symbols and calculations expressed in their own scripts.

MAKING THE GAME LESS COMPLEX

Sometimes a game seems more difficult to play than it really is because of the way the rules are worded. This can be dealt with by rewriting them more clearly. Suggestions on how to write clear instructions and rules are made on page 96. This section is more concerned with ways of simplifying what actually happens during play. Many published games introduce complications and extra stages that may make them hard to follow for non-native speakers of a language, who are not familiar with the original game. Sometimes even native speakers have to spend too much time between turns, consulting the rules and wondering what to do next. Very often it is possible to simplify the game. For example, rules for scoring are often too complex. Many games require players to add on bonus points and take off penalties in a rather complicated way. This probably adds little to the amount of language used and slows down play and confuses the students. These complications can be reduced by forgetting penalties and bonuses and by having players count up their raw scores only.

SHORTENING THE GAME

Some games in their original version simply last too long for foreign students to be able to finish them within a normal class session. Any game that calls for facility with things like vocabulary or spelling will naturally be played at a slower rate by non-native speakers. *Scrabble,* for example, is a game that normally finishes when all the letter tiles in the set have been used up, or when no one can make a new word with any of the remaining tiles. This stage may take one or two hours for native speakers to reach so foreign students are unlikely to finish the game in the time available. In a game which, like *Scrabble,* proceeds in a number of rounds in which each player has a turn, you can change the rules so that the game ends after a certain number of rounds (say, five). Scores or advantages can be calculated at this point to decide upon the winner.

6.2 Inventing games

Someone who is designing a language game from scratch has quite a difficult task. He has to create something that not only works as a game but also stimulates a significant amount of language. It is a good thing if the structures or functions that will most frequently be used in a game are predictable. This allows the game to be fitted into the appropriate place in a course. A game that leads to random talk is not much use.

Chapter 1 gave some of the ways in which games can be won – finishing first, collecting more of something, being the last one left in, finding the answer to a puzzle, etc – and some of the ways in which players succeed in non-competitive games – by giving and following instructions that lead to the completion of something, for example. This information is summarised in Figure 3, on page 7. Chapter 5 emphasised the importance of the right interaction pattern of players to match the type of language practice needed at a particular time. It is important to keep these factors in mind when following the 'game-maker's recipe' which appears below. The numbers in Figure 13 identify the steps taken in this example, which shows how a game might be made.

1 I need a game to help my students practise a function – warning.

2 I am more interested in their using this function to change their colleagues' behaviour than in the details of structure and pronunciation. They will have had ample practice in the language lab and in class drills by now.

3 I therefore want a communication game.

4 Warning suggests that one person is trying to help another, so perhaps a game involving cooperation between the players is appropriate.

5 I shall therefore look at information-exchange games.

6 An appropriate goal might be for one player to complete a journey.

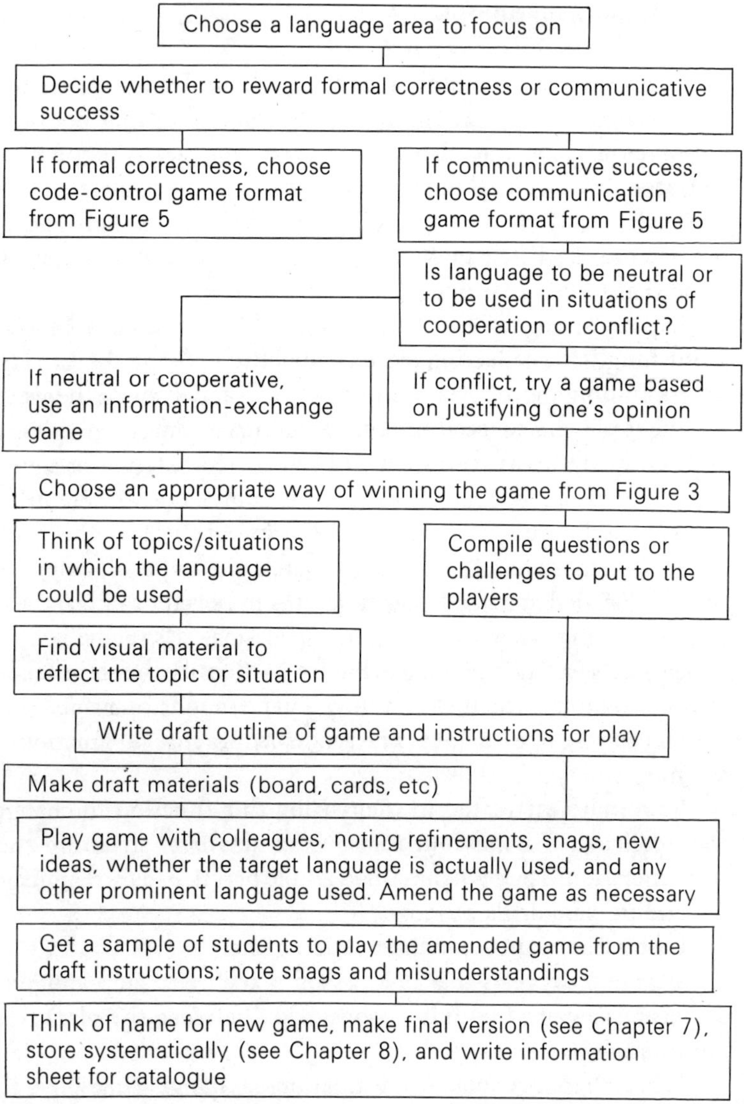

Figure 13 Steps in inventing a game

7 On the way, he could consult his partner, who knows about dangers on the way.

8 Maps or plans would be appropriate, plus small pictures of hazards that can be put onto the maps. Should the subject matter be everyday (eg traffic maps) or less common (eg jungle or desert island)? Try all three possibilities.

9 Try having two players. One knows nothing about the dangers of the terrain, but the other is in a position to find out and warn him. Each player has an identical map, but player A has a number of Danger cards which he puts face down, at random on his map. Player B is trying to get from one point to another, and there are several possible routes. He tells player A which way he is going, and player A warns him about nearby dangers by turning over the Danger card as player B nears the places on his route which are close to them. The two players cannot see each other's maps, of course.

10 The materials in draft look something like Figure 14.

11 I try materials with two colleagues. Immediate problems:

i Player A puts his cards down in such a way that it is impossible for B ever to reach his destination. Every way is blocked by some terrible danger. *Solution:* Mark the places on the map where cards may be put down, so that there is always a possible route left open.

ii Players A and B do not always know whether they are referring to the same bit of the map, however carefully they describe their location. *Solution:* Put in a number of 'landmarks' on both maps, eg a large pine tree, a lake or a ruined castle.

iii Player B complains that *he* is not using any of the warning language that the game is designed to practise. This is true, but he is listening and responding to it. *Partial solution:* Make players change places after the first game, rearrange the danger cards and play it again.

The new materials, after emendation, are as in Figure 15.

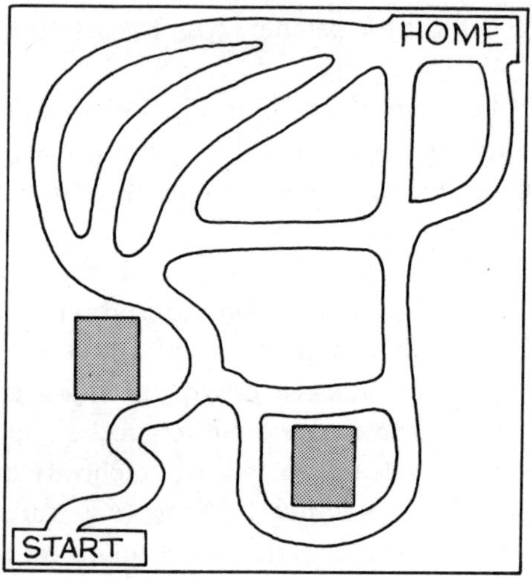

Player A (the warner)

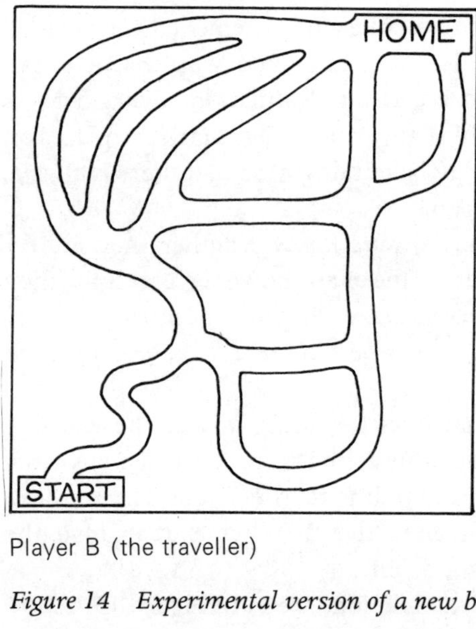

Player B (the traveller)

Danger cards

Figure 14 Experimental version of a new board game

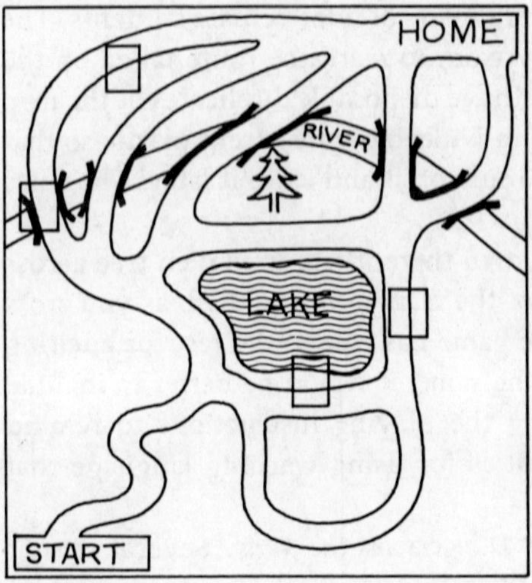

Player A

□ = place where Player A may put a danger card

Danger cards

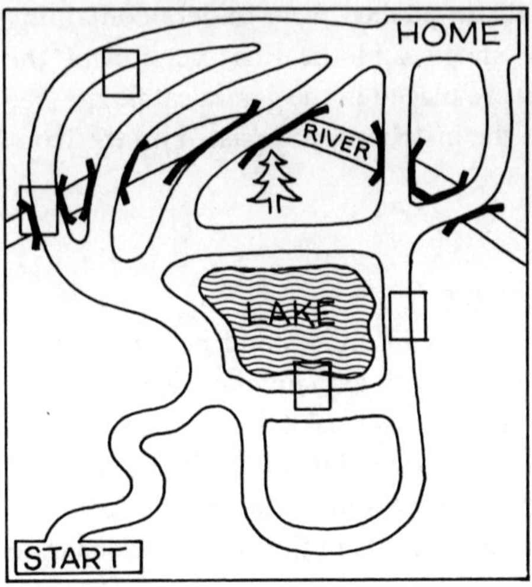

Player B

Figure 15   Final version of a new board game

12 I try the game on several pairs of intermediate students. The main problem is that they want to mark the route taken on the map itself. *Solution:* either have disposable duplicates of the map or (better) cover one map in wipeable transparent plastic so that the student can draw his route on it and erase it later. The rules were well understood.

Language like 'Don't go down there, there is a fallen tree across the road' and 'Be careful of the man-eating goldfish as you cross the lake' was used. So the game has passed the test for eliciting the language I want. All the same, it would be better to include the language focus among the playing instructions to remind students of the opportunities for using warning language that this game gives them.

13 I shall call the game *Dangers on the Way*. Several sets of maps are drawn and placed in folders. Plastic-covered versions are made for player B to trace his route on. The Danger cards are put in an envelope with the map. This is a new game so the folders need to be easily distinguished from folders containing other games. Information sheets and the final version of the instructions (see Figure 16) are placed in the games catalogue (see Section 8.1), and a copy of the instructions is pasted on the front of the folder.

WRITING INSTRUCTIONS

No game will succeed if no one can understand how to play it. Although it is always a good idea to explain and demonstrate a new game yourself, you should also make sure that there are clear, unambiguous, written instructions for colleagues and students to refer to. The golden rules for clear instructions are:

1 Break down the sequence of events in the game into separate steps.
2 Number each step separately.
3 Keep sentences fairly short.

DANGERS ON THE WAY

(2 players)

INSTRUCTIONS FOR PLAYER A

Do not open this folder until you have read the instructions below:

1 In this folder you will find two maps: give the one marked B to Player B.

2 Take map A yourself. Do not let Player B see your map.

3 Take the envelope marked Danger Cards. You can put five of these on any of the squares marked on your map. Do not let Player B see how you have positioned them.

4 Player B must trace a route from Start to Home. Watch him as he does this and warn him when he is coming close to any danger that you have placed on your map.

5 Player B must find another way when his path is blocked by a danger.

6 See how quickly you can guide B safely to Home.

Figure 16 Instructions for the game invented in this chapter

4 Do not refer vaguely to 'the first player', 'the second player', etc: it is clearer to label them 'A', 'B', etc, and refer to them as such throughout.

5 Make it absolutely clear what the players have to do in order to win.

Options include suggestions on the sort of language that would

DESCRIBE AND ARRANGE

(2 players)

INSTRUCTIONS FOR PLAYER A

Do not open this folder until you have read the instructions below:

1 In this folder you will find a picture. Do not show this picture to Player B.

2 You will also find an envelope with a set of small pictures in it. Give these pictures to Player B.

3 Player B's small pictures make up your picture when arranged in order. Tell Player B how to arrange his pictures in the same way. Tell him he may ask you questions.

4 When Player B has finished arranging his pictures, show him your picture. Compare the two arrangements and discuss any language difficulties.

Figure 17 Examples of written instructions

be useful in the game, and a request to count any pieces and to tidy up when the game is over! For games where it is essential to start with an information gap, make sure that there is a warning at the beginning of the instructions not to look at one's partner's materials.

Figure 17 shows some examples of clearly written instructions.

DESCRIBE AND DRAW

(2 players)

INSTRUCTIONS FOR PLAYER A

Do not open this folder until you have read the instructions below:

1 In the folder you will find a picture. Do not show the picture to Player B.

2 Player B needs a pencil, a rubber and some paper.

3 Describe the picture to Player B. You may give him a general description of the picture first. Tell Player B to draw what you describe. He may ask you questions.

4 When Player B has finished drawing, show him your picture. Compare the two pictures and discuss any differences.

FIND THE DIFFERENCE

(2 players)

INSTRUCTIONS FOR PLAYERS A & B

Do not open this folder until you have read the instructions below:

1 In this folder you will find 2 envelopes. Take one each.

2 There is a picture in each envelope. Do not show it to the other player.

3 Your picture is similar to that of the other player, but there are some differences. Talk to one another until you find four differences.

4 When you have found four differences, show your pictures to one another and compare them. Try to find more differences.

7 Materials for games

This chapter deals with the materials you will need for some of the games mentioned elsewhere in the book – how to make them attractive to look at, easy to use, and not likely to fall to pieces too quickly.

Figure 18 gives a list of materials and equipment you are likely to need. The left-hand column shows the basic items, most of which should be already available in schools. The column on the right shows things that a school with more money to spare could add to or substitute for the items on the basic list. Some indication of the function of each thing is given on the lists, but further notes on their uses will appear below.

The basic techniques involved in making games – cutting, sticking, reinforcing – and in choosing suitable visual material to start with are probably best illustrated by taking actual games from this book and describing, step by step, how they are made, commenting on different choices that can be made according to how much time and money is available, and noting how the appearance of the materials can affect the success of the games. There is a lot of practical help and guidance on the production of materials in another book in this series, *Look Here! A Visual Aids Handbook for Language Teachers* by Betty Morgan Bowen.

7.1 Games with cards

Visual prompts like small word or picture cards not only are attractive but also influence turn-taking in a game. Having each

Basic	De luxe
ruler	
straight edge of metal for use with razor blade	
razor blade or Stanley knife large scissors	office guillotine
glue and paste	
lead pencil eraser carbon paper for tracing pictures making copies of instructions, etc	photocopier typewriter stencils and duplicating machine
tracing paper stapler and staples	
biros in various colours coloured pencils felt-tipped pens	
clear Sellotape cloth-backed adhesive tape	transparent plastic film for protecting surfaces
heavy card light card	coloured index cards, blank visiting cards, etc
poster paints and brushes	A4-sized cardboard folders in several colours
small objects for printing with (potatoes, pieces of balsa wood, etc)	child's printing set and ink pads
typing paper for making labels and master sheets for instructions	Letraset or other rub-off letters and numbers
old magazines, catalogues, etc to use as source of pictures	small stick-on coloured labels in various shapes (the type that is sold in sheets) for use in colour coding
	stencils of letters and numbers.
	child's stencils of common objects.
	dice plastic counters

Figure 18 Equipment and materials for making games

player take a card is one way of making sure that each person in a game has a turn in which he leads the group and that opportunities to speak are evenly distributed. Cards, of course, also give students something to talk about. Without such physical means of structuring moves and providing subject matter, students left to themselves can find that some members of the group dominate, or that there are long silences while everybody tries to think whose turn it is. Two examples of games in which players mark the beginning or the end of a turn by doing something with a card and talking about what they have done are *Picture Dominoes* and *What's the Word?*

The most important thing to decide is how big the cards should be. They should be convenient to hold but large enough for the words or pictures on them to be seen by several people at one time if necessary. If you already have some pieces of card, such as index cards, which are rather too big, it is more economical to see if they can simply be cut in half or quarters than to trim them down to some predetermined size. Once you have fixed a size, cut a good supply of cards plus some spares for replacements.

Cards that belong in the same pack should if possible be the same colour to indicate that they belong together, and they should have an identification mark on the back to indicate which game they belong to. Writing or drawing on the backs of thirty or more cards can be laborious. It is quicker and more attractive to use some sort of printing device. A child's printing set allows you to print the full title of the game, but you can use any small flat object with a distinctive shape to print a symbol – the flat end of a pencil for example. Alternatively you can cut your own design onto a lino block, the flat surface of a cut potato or even an old rubber eraser. Do not forget that if you cut out letters or numbers they must be reversed on the block if they are to print the right way round. You can use an ink pad or thick poster paint to print with. Figure 19 shows this technique.

The cards are now ready to have the words or pictures put on

Simple design drawn on cut face of potato, etc

Surrounding material cut away

Design inked up

Design stamped on game

Figure 19 Printing with a cut potato

the fronts. For a word game such as *What's the Word?* it is easy enough to write the different words by hand. A fine-tipped permanent marker makes a clearer outline than biro, but most types of ordinary felt-tipped pen have a tendency to smudge if the cards are handled constantly. Biro is fainter but more permanent. Words could of course also be typed on to cards but this is extremely time-consuming.

The pictures needed for games like *Picture Dominoes* can be obtained in a number of ways. They can be cut from old magazines or mail-order catalogues (ideal when small pictures are needed) and glued on. They can be drawn freehand or traced in outline from illustrations in books. It is best to choose pictures of single objects and to cut them away from any distracting background (see Figure 20). The result should be clear enough to be recognised even by a player who has to look at a card upside-down because of where he is sitting in the group. Preparation of the cards could stop at this point, but they could be covered with plastic film (see Figure 21) to protect them from the effects of handling. Using a laminating machine makes the job much simpler and quicker although this is definitely for institutions with 'de luxe' facilities.

Principal object cut from its background. Good colour contrast with card. Object has a distinctive shape.

Object is unclear because it has not been cut away from its background. Insufficient contrast and clarity of outline. It is uncertain which the important aspect of this scene is.

Figure 20 Choosing suitable pictures

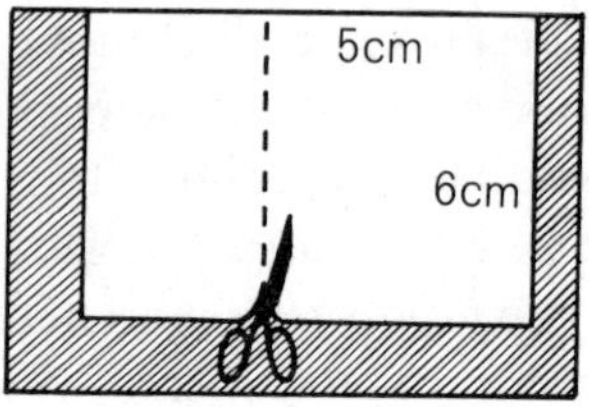

Card cut to size

Picture cut out and stuck on card

Transparent plastic film laid over card and the corners cut off

Plastic film folded over to back of card

Figure 21 *Making small cards*

7.2 Communication games for pairs

One of the important principles behind communication games is the information gap. This means that the game should start with one player having a different set of information from another. It is therefore an essential part of the game that information should be secret at the beginning. If players pick up the materials and can see the answer immediately the whole point of playing it is lost. The physical design of the material should ensure that this does not happen. The different materials for each player should be kept separately in small envelopes or cardboard folders so that each will not be able to see what the other person has. A con-

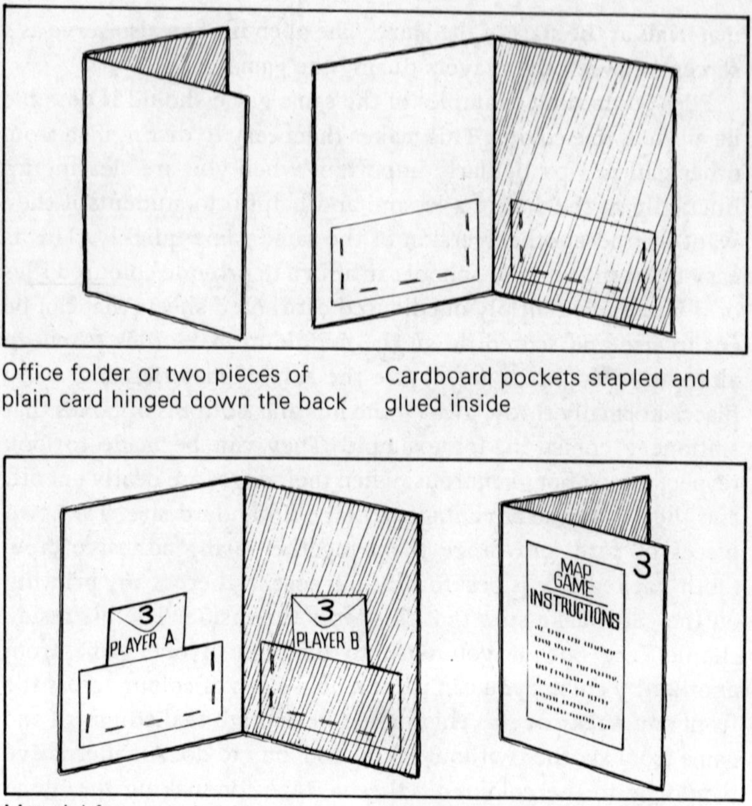

Office folder or two pieces of plain card hinged down the back

Cardboard pockets stapled and glued inside

Material for game held in place in pockets

Instructions and title pasted onto front of folder; each folder has its own number, also written on accompanying materials.

Figure 22 Making a folder for a pair or small-group game

venient way of holding them is to use a simple cardboard office file. Inside this you can glue and staple pockets made of light card, as shown in Figure 22, which will hold the materials. The instructions for the game can be pasted on the front cover of the file along with a warning not to look at the other player's materials at the start of the game. The open file can also serve as a screen between the players during the game.

Files containing examples of the same game should if possible be all the same colour. This makes them easy to distinguish from other games – particularly important when you are clearing up hurriedly at the end of a lesson, and helpful to students if they want to find another version of the same game quickly. This is easy to arrange if your school can afford to provide coloured files or if you have a supply of coloured cardboard sheets that can be cut to size and scored down the middle to make files. A cheap alternative might be to recycle the sort of material that many places normally throw away – the lids and bottoms of boxes that stationery comes in, for example. They can be made to look respectable, if not glamorous, when their edges are neatly cut off, and they have the advantage of being a standard size. Take two pieces of card and hinge them together using adhesive tape. Cloth-backed tape is best for this purpose. If there is any printing on the card make sure that this faces the inside. The plain side should face out. If you wish to distinguish one game from another by colour you can paint a bold slash of colour across the front and back covers. This should be enough to distinguish one game from another without taking too long to do. An alternative would be to use coloured adhesive tape for making the hinge between the two pieces of card.

The title of each game and the instructions for play should be put onto the front of each file. It is most convenient to keep duplicate sets of instructions so that one can be pasted on to each new copy of the game as it is made. These could be duplicated by cutting a stencil or by photocopying from a master sheet. The most economical use of stencil and duplicating paper would be to fit instructions for two or more different games on to one sheet. The sheets can then be cut across with a guillotine. If a photocopier is used you can achieve a bolder effect by using Letraset or similar rub-off letters for the title of the game.

7.3 Board games

A game board should be as stoutly made as possible if it is to lie flat without curling and to survive repeated use (see Figure 23). It should be as large as possible, since the pictures or writing on it will have to be large enough to be clearly visible to all the players sitting around it. Heavy card is expensive, but again you could find a cheap substitute in materials that might otherwise be thrown away, especially since most of the surface of the board will be covered with stuck-on paper pictures from magazines and other sources. This means that the drab basic appearance of waste cardboard need not prevent the board from looking attractive. Two sheets of thin card can be glued together to make a thicker, heavier board. Game boards should fold in two for easy storage and to protect the inner playing surface, so you will need two separate pieces of card hinged together. It is usually better to draw the design on each of the two halves before you reinforce the joint on the inside of the board. Use transparent tape for this and put it on over the design.

Most board games involve players moving around a track drawn on the board. This track can either be continuous, with players going round again and again (the board for *Monopoly* is an example of this in a published game) or it can be a track with a beginning and an end. In the latter type of game, such as *If*, the players are usually racing to get to the end of the board first. Other boards allow players to choose between branching paths. Still others can be based on maps or charts and their layout will of course depend on the original source. Some suggested layouts for boards are shown in Figure 24.

The track on a board is usually divided into small sections. Players move a number of spaces forwards or backwards along the track during each turn. If you want to make the overall shape of the track clearer and the board more attractive you can paint the parts surrounding the track a different colour. For outlining

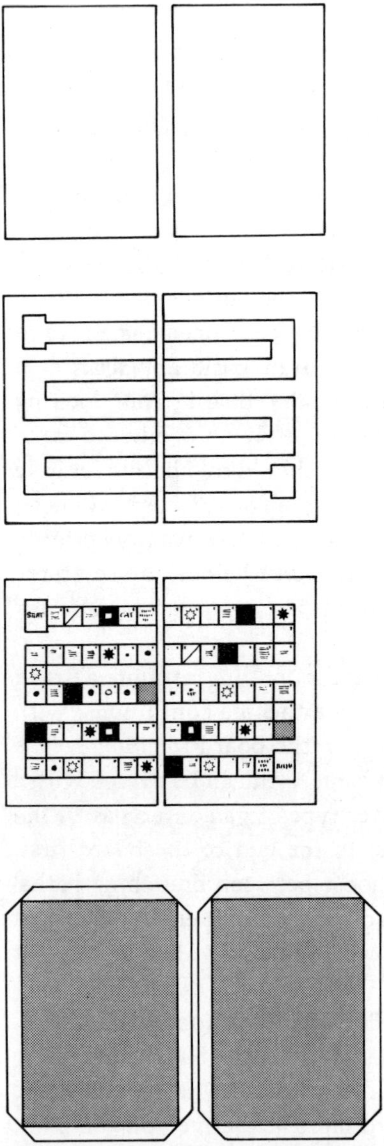

1 Two pieces of stout card

2 Design of track carefully drawn on and matched up; background painted if wished

3 Pictures or words drawn or cut out and stuck on divisions of the track

4 Each half covered separately with oversize plastic film, and the corners of the film cut off

Figure 23 Making a board game

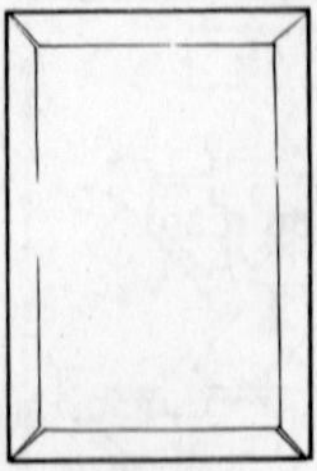

5 The film folded over to the back of each half of the board.

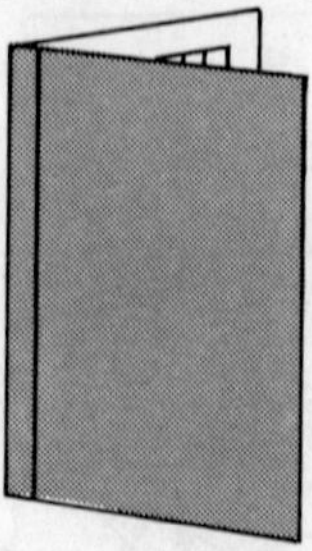

6 The two halves hinged together on the reverse side, using strong adhesive tape

7 A slight gap left between the two halves to allow easy folding

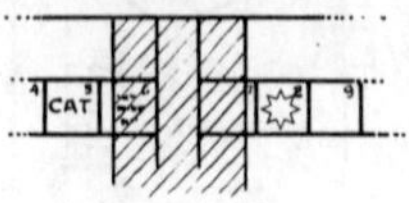

8 Hinge reinforced if necessary on the right side of the board using transparent adhesive tape

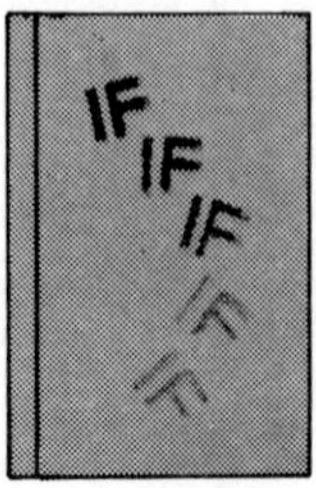

9 Reverse side of board decorated with distinctive symbols to identify the game —printed using potato-cut technique (see Figure 19)

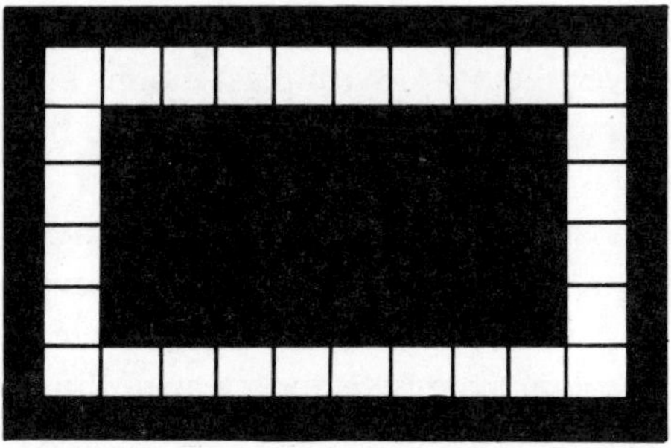

Continuous track

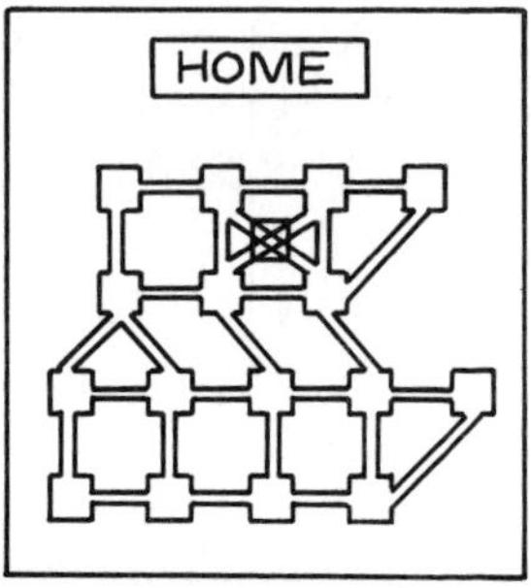

Branching paths

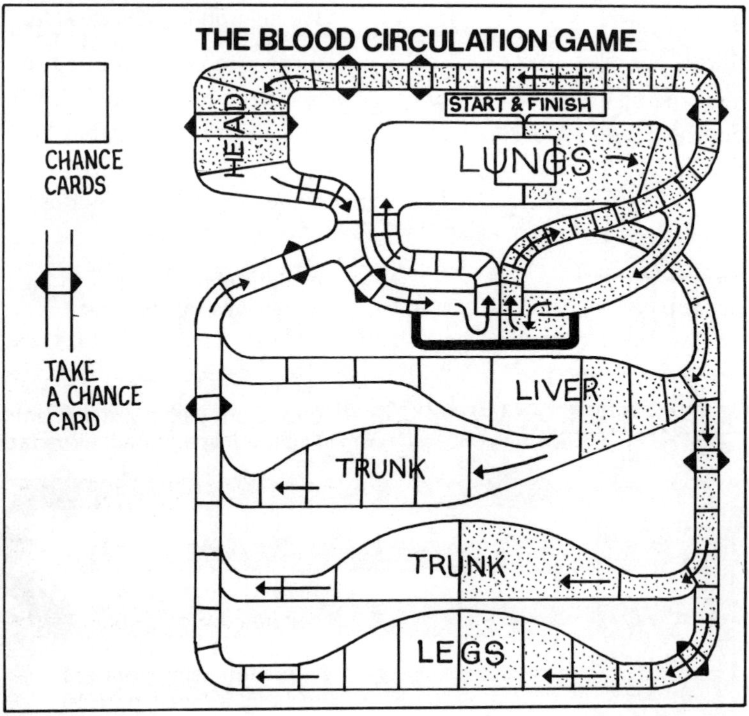

A 'realistic' track

Figure 24 Layouts for boards

the track and its divisions, avoid inks that will run or smudge, especially if you intend to cover the board with plastic film. The ink from felt-tipped pens, in particular, tends to 'bleed' into the plastic eventually, producing a strange, fuzzy effect.

When the track and its divisions have been drawn, the next step is to put in the pictures, numbers, instructions or whatever else is needed on the board. Aim at a bold effect which is clear from several angles. Strong colour contrasts and clear outlines around pictures will make them more attractive and recognisable. If you wish to cover the board with plastic film it is better to cover each half separately before the two are hinged together. This prevents the plastic wrinkling at the point where the board folds over, and also gives you a smaller area to cover at one time since using adhesive film on large areas is not at all easy. This is another case where a laminating machine saves trouble and guarantees a presentable result.

Once the board has reached this stage it needs some identification on the back so that it can be easily found amongst the other boards. This could be written, or printed on as suggested in Section 7.1.

Many board games need small tokens to mark each player's progress around the board. These can be bought or cheaply made out of differently coloured pieces of card. Dice are often needed, too, but they will have to be bought if they are to fall without

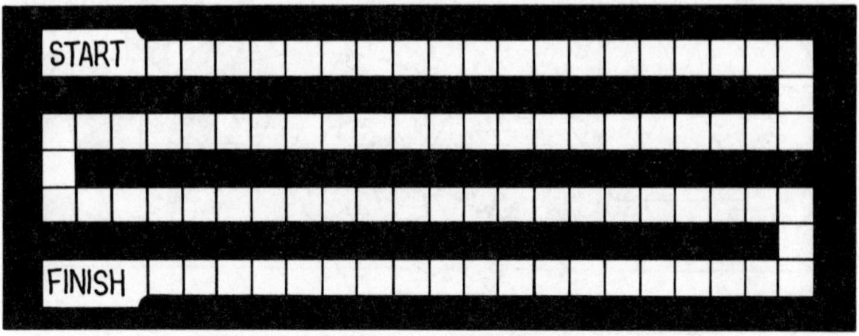

'Beginning-and-end' track

bias. Home-made dice never work very well. Dice can however be substituted by spinners or other devices for arriving at a number by chance. Figure 25 shows how to make a spinner. You can put what you like in the segments of the spinner – numbers or perhaps instructions about how to move (see Figure 26). Another way of deciding moves is to write instructions or numbers on small pieces of card for players to pick up at random.

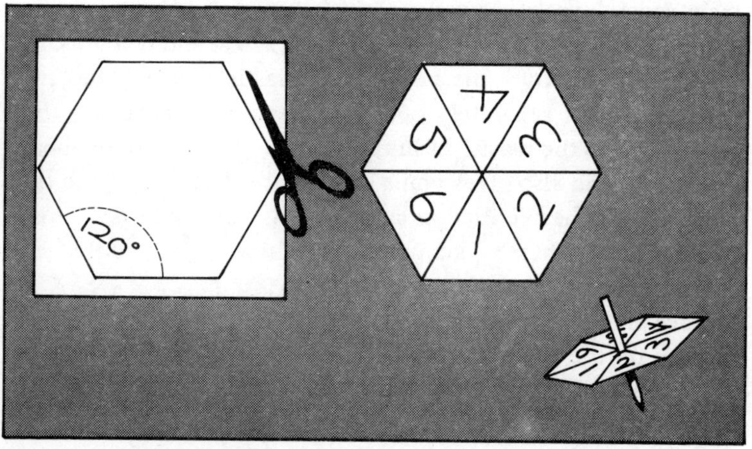

Figure 25 How to make a spinner

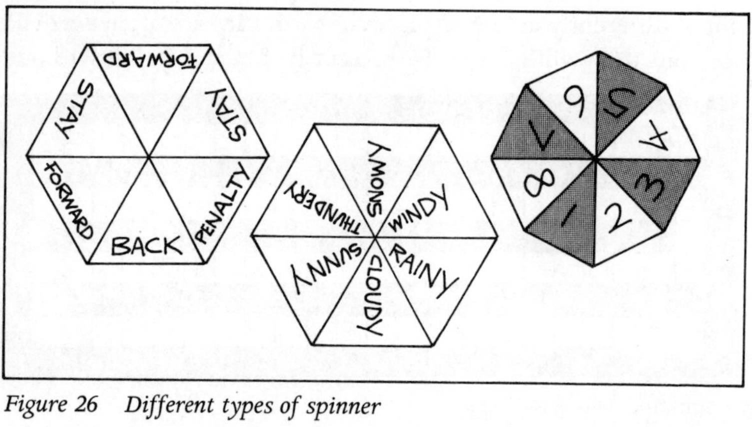

Figure 26 Different types of spinner

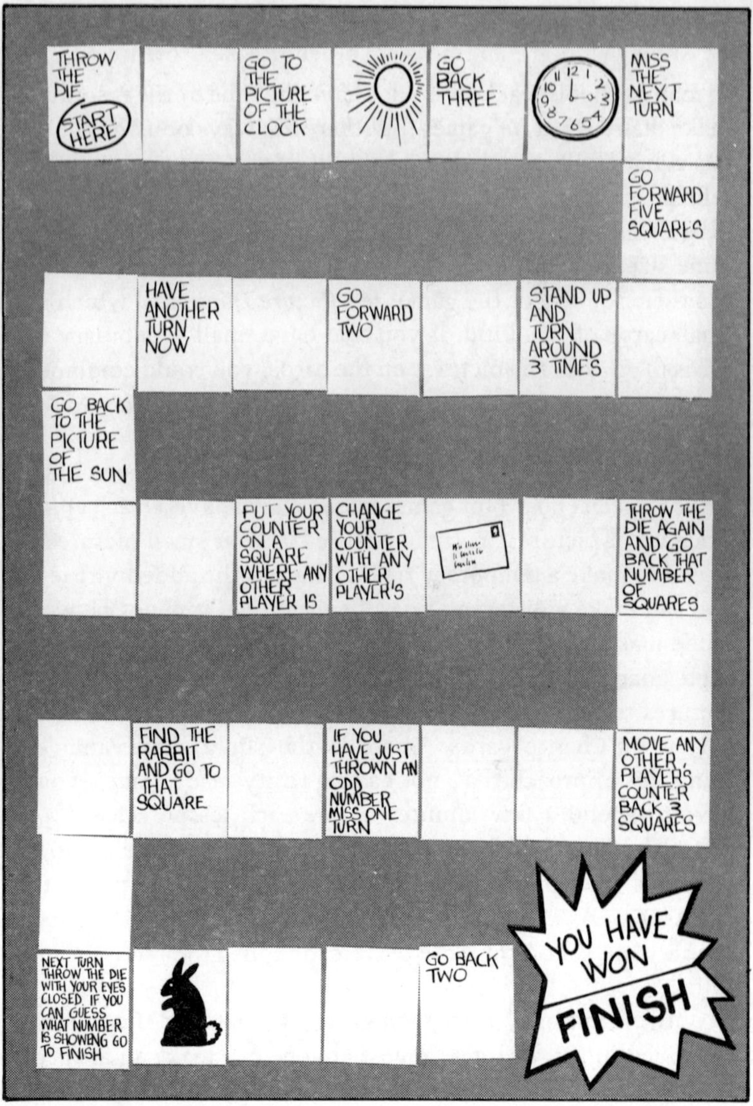

Figure 27 *Do As You Are Told, a 'board' game made from multi-purpose cards*

7.4 Multi-purpose materials

In many schools teachers do not have the time or the resources to make many separate games, but there are ways of using the same basic materials again and again to make 'temporary' games, which can be used once and then dismantled. If for example you plan ahead so that all your small picture cards are more or less the same size, you can easily make a selection from your stock and use them for any of the games (eg *Picture Dominoes*) which need small cards of this kind. If you also have small vocabulary flash cards to go with the pictures on the cards, you could combine the two to make temporary versions of games like *Snap* and *Pelmanism*.

If you have a large surface to play on you do not even have to make a special board for games like *If* which have a track entirely made up of pictures. You can simply lay your small pictures end to end to make a temporary track. This has the added virtue that you can make a different 'board' every time. It might be worthwhile making a few standard-sized instruction cards to go with such board games, which could either be mixed in with the pictures to form part of the track or kept in a pile to be used as Forfeit or Chance cards. There is the slight disadvantage in using this approach that, not having ready-made games, you do have to spend a few minutes before each lesson selecting the materials from which to build your game, but the saving in materials and preparation time may well make up for this. *Do As You Are Told* (see Figure 27) illustrates this idea. It is a simple game for one or more players, designed to practise reading skills.

With enthusiasm, a few very basic materials and the processes described in this chapter, almost anyone can make an attractive and effective game.

8 Organising a collection

If you are going to use language games frequently you need to have a large number of them easily available. You also need to be able to find what you want quickly and easily. It is therefore important, in all but the very smallest teaching institutions, to work out some system for classifying and, where necessary, storing your games. From this practical point of view there are two kinds of game: those which have special materials like cards, boards, dice, etc, which need to be stored, and those which present no storage problem because they are played with nothing more than what is already available in the classroom – blackboard and chalk and so on.

Naturally the second kind of game will be attractive to most teachers, but it would be a pity to restrict a collection to these 'no-materials' games. The main reason is that most of them have to be played under the teacher's control. This is not a bad thing in itself, but it does mean that by using only this kind of game you have greatly limited the variety of interactions and activities that you can set up by using games. As soon as you start using games in which materials like picture cards act as prompts to guide what the players do and say, you create the possibility of activities in which the students are more independent of the teacher and which they can do in pairs or small groups. This not only provides more variety but also allows students to develop the language skills needed for face-to-face communication. So even though it may mean a little extra trouble, it is worthwhile keeping a store of materials that can be used for this type of game.

8.1 Keeping a games catalogue

Whether or not you have physical materials for a game on your shelves, you should make sure that it is recorded somehow, so that the rules and instructions for playing it are available to anyone who might want to use it in their teaching. This can be done in a number of ways. Some teachers keep an 'ideas box' with descriptions of games on index cards, but perhaps a more convenient way of storing this information, if more than one member of staff is going to look at it, is to use a large loose-leaf file with a separate page for each game. New games can be added as they are discovered or invented.

How detailed the descriptions of games need to be depends very much on who is using the catalogue. If only two or three teachers are working closely together, it can be used mainly as an aide-memoire and the descriptions can be fairly brief. On the other hand, if there is a large teaching staff and not all of them are familiar with using games, then instructions and comments on the catalogue will have to be very explicit. One of the essential things is for the user to be able to see immediately what language areas a game will provide practice in. Some books of games divide the games up according to the language items or skills that are most prominent. However it is hard to describe a game adequately in this way. A language skill, like listening for detail, might be just as important a feature in a game as the grammatical structure it seems to focus upon. The simplest solution might be to make the major divisions in the catalogue according to the main skills you want to teach, but to ensure that the information sheets themselves make the other language features of the games sufficiently prominent. Categories such as reading games, writing games, spelling games, pronunciation games and listening comprehension games cover many games quite adequately. Both code-control and communication games can be found under each category, since they can deal with the same areas of language.

It is more convenient to have them grouped together like this than kept in separate parts of the catalogue.

You may wish, if your collection of games is large, to index the games in your catalogue in any number of ways: according to the structures practised, for example, or the language functions most often used in communication games. What information you focus on depends very much on the needs and interests of each set of teachers, but the important thing is to do the minimum necessary to keep everyone adequately informed. The games will not improve in quality by being intricately and elaborately catalogued just for the sake of it!

Figure 28 shows how one of the information sheets in the catalogue might look. It is a modification of the way in which games described in this book have been presented. Its main aim is to display information in such a way that a teacher hurriedly looking through the catalogue can pick out the information he needs without having to read all the way through a densely written page. Each category of information appears in the same position on each sheet, and where appropriate, symbols are used to save reading time. Two spots could indicate a pair game, for example, a square a game for small groups, and two parallel lines a game for two teams. An indication of the length of time each game takes to play should always be given so that the teacher can tell whether it will fit into the lesson he plans to give. If special materials are needed for a game they should be listed and their location in the storage system clearly given. Cross-references to similar games are also useful to include on this sheet. The description on the information sheet gives an outline of what happens during play and is there to give potential users the general 'flavour' of the game. There is a space underneath this for members of staff to give first-hand information about problems encountered or extra possibilities for use that they discover.

The actual rules and instructions for play are best kept on a separate sheet filed next to the information sheet. The reason for

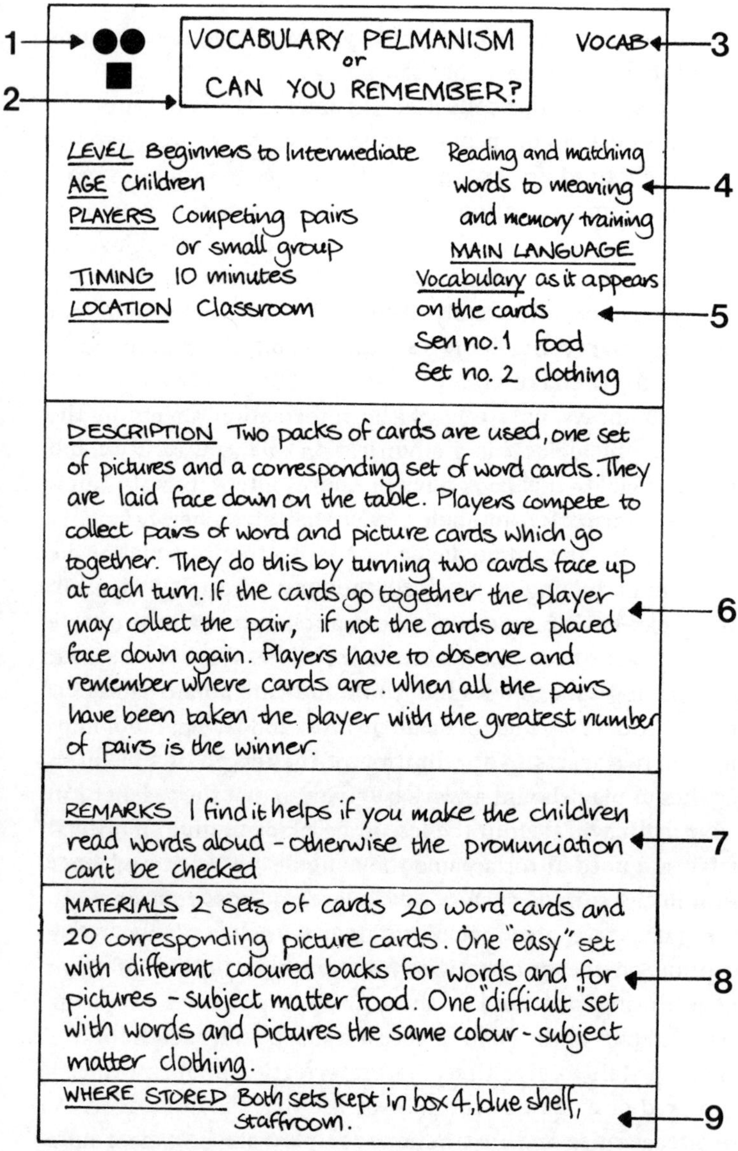
1 ●● ■

2 VOCABULARY PELMANISM or CAN YOU REMEMBER?

VOCAB 3

LEVEL Beginners to Intermediate

AGE Children

PLAYERS Competing pairs or small group

TIMING 10 minutes

LOCATION Classroom

Reading and matching words to meaning and memory training 4

MAIN LANGUAGE

Vocabulary as it appears on the cards 5

Set no. 1 food

Set no. 2 clothing

DESCRIPTION Two packs of cards are used, one set of pictures and a corresponding set of word cards. They are laid face down on the table. Players compete to collect pairs of word and picture cards which go together. They do this by turning two cards face up at each turn. If the cards go together the player may collect the pair, if not the cards are placed face down again. Players have to observe and remember where cards are. When all the pairs have been taken the player with the greatest number of pairs is the winner. 6

REMARKS I find it helps if you make the children read words aloud - otherwise the pronunciation can't be checked 7

MATERIALS 2 sets of cards 20 word cards and 20 corresponding picture cards. One "easy" set with different coloured backs for words and for pictures - subject matter food. One "difficult" set with words and pictures the same colour - subject matter clothing. 8

WHERE STORED Both sets kept in box 4, blue shelf, staffroom. 9

Figure 28 Information sheet for use in a games catalogue

1 Quickly seen symbols to mean a game for a pair or a small group
2 Box for title
3 Short heading giving main focus; more details given below
4 Description of skills used in game
5 Language area
6 Details on play
7 Space for teachers to write in remarks and hints on play
8 Description of the materials
9 Note on where the materials are kept

this is that it is not easy to get an overall picture of what a game is like to play by reading its rules alone. These have to be very precisely worded and often turn out rather flavourless. It is much better for someone new to a game to read the description on the information sheet, decide whether he likes the sound of it, and *then* turn to the rules if he wishes to know more. Suggestions on writing clear unambiguous rules are given on page 96.

Following these suggestions means that someone needs to take general charge of organising the catalogue, encouraging other members of staff to write up new games, making sure that a supply of information sheets is available, and so on. For some institutions it may be enough to provide blank sheets of paper, with guidelines about how the information should be set out kept in the front of the catalogue, but if you have duplicating facilities of any kind it would be a good idea to design an information form with the main headings already provided. New supplies of these forms can then be run off as necessary. All of this presupposes that teachers work together or at least cooperate to some extent. Where this is not so, an arrangement that starts informally among a few members of staff for a limited aim could be the start of more widespread cooperation.

8.2 Storing and organising materials

It is a good idea to have a special area in the staff room or store room where games are kept. Deep bookshelves make very convenient storage since the games are more visible and accessible than if they are kept in a cupboard. A large map chest also makes a good storage place. Each game should have its own place, to which it is returned after being used. The most important thing is that each game should have its own container and that the container should be strong and clearly labelled. If this is so they can survive even being piled up in a corner if there is no other storage space.

The most suitable type of container depends on the game (see Figure 29). Cardboard boxes with lids are useful for games that consist of several different types of material. Cards, tokens and other pieces can be kept tidily in their own envelopes inside the box. Stand-up open loose files are very suitable for holding the

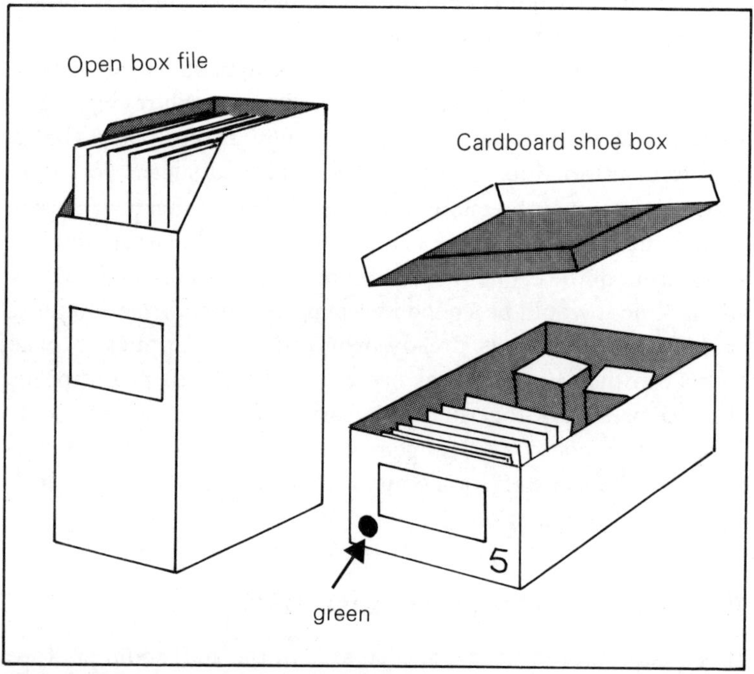

Figure 29 Containers for games

type of games that are mounted in cardboard folders. Each file will take about twenty folders, which is enough for a class set of one pair game. Each container should have a list of its contents glued somewhere on it, since this makes checking for missing pieces much easier.

Where there are many examples of the same game, as should be the case with games such as *Find the Difference* or *Describe and Draw,* all the versions of any one game should be the same colour, there should also be a simple index of the subject matter of the pictures in each folder. Each folder should have its own number on the outside cover so that it will be easy for the teacher to locate a particular version in the index and then find the folder with the appropriate number (see Figure 30). So, for example, he would know that the *Find the Difference* game using contrasting pictures of, say, women's hats is in folder number 19, but that the two pictures of dogs are in folder number 8 in the same container. It is also good to code the different versions of a game according to their relative difficulty by means of, say, between one and five coloured spots on the front of each folder, as in Figure 30.

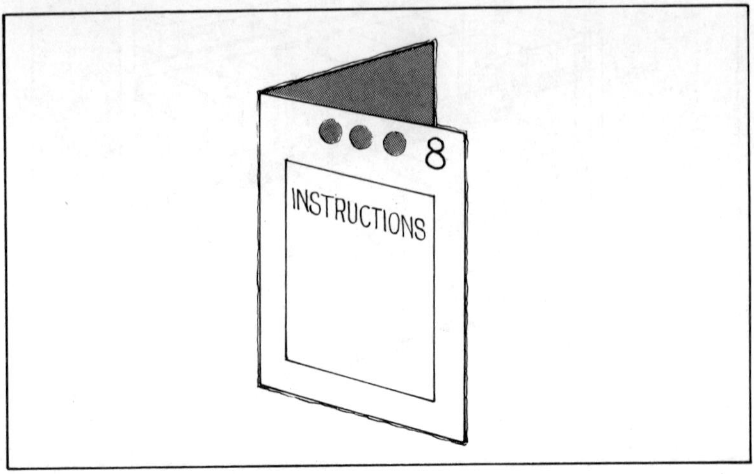

Figure 30 Folder for a pair game

All games should have sets of instructions with them. These should be duplicates of the instruction sheets that are kept in the catalogue of games. Games that are mounted inside folders should have a set of instructions pasted on to the front cover of each folder. Other games should have instructions enclosed in each box. If these are mounted on thin card and covered with plastic film (see Figure 21 on page 106), they will stand up better to constant handling.

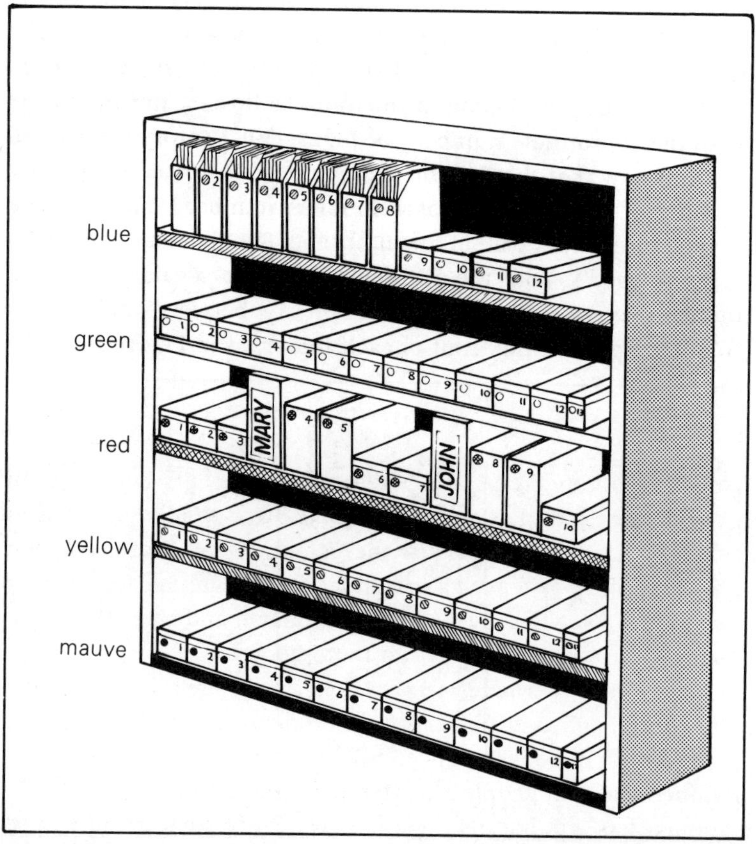

Figure 31 Games cabinet

The location of each game in the storage system should be given on the information sheets in the catalogue, even if it is only something like 'on the windowsill next to the filing cabinet', but where possible an exact location on a set of shelves should be given. If there are many games in the collection you will need a shelf plan, to be fixed somewhere near the shelves, with a copy kept in the front of the games catalogue. The correct place for each box or other container should be clearly indicated on this plan. If you mark your shelves and your containers with matching colours it will be much easier to locate a game or to see at a glance if something is out of its proper place (see Figure 31). Each shelf or drawer has a coloured strip stuck along its edge, and the boxes that belong on that shelf or in that drawer have small sticky labels of the same colour stuck onto them. The boxes are numbered to indicate their position from left to right on the shelf or in the drawer, with the numbers written on the coloured labels. The shoe box shown in Figure 29 is number 5 on the green shelf.

8.3 Organising the borrowing of games

How can you avoid a clash between two teachers who want to use the same materials at the same time? One simple system is to pin up a blank timetable for the coming week. Teachers who know that they will need a particular set of materials for a lesson can then book them by writing their name and the title of the game in the appropriate slot on the timetable.

Every time some materials are taken from a shelf, whether they have been booked or not, it should be clear who has taken them. A signing-out book or sheet is a possibility, but it is rather cumbersome and people are often tempted not to bother with it. A much less troublesome method is to have some small empty boxes which have teachers' names prominently marked on one side. Whenever a teacher takes something from the shelves he should put 'his' box in the space left behind. Since this involves almost no trouble at all it is likely that staff will be conscientious about keeping to the rule. A glance at the shelves will then tell you who has currently got the materials in their possession (see Figure 31).

If you are providing games for students to use as a facility in a student resources centre, you need to do as much as you can to help students find what they want, and, just as important, to put it back again in the right place so that others can find it. Although there is usually a teacher on duty, his function is to help people with language, not to sort out disorganised materials. Labelling shelves and games and colour-coding them as suggested before is helpful, although the students will need, of course, to be shown how to use the system when looking for games or putting them back. Students do not need a detailed catalogue of games to help them choose. A simple list of titles, with notes on the language that can be practised through the game, and an indication of the number of players it needs should be enough. Each game on the list should have its shelf or drawer indicated next to it, and a shelf plan with all the games marked on it will guide students to the right place.

If the suggestions about identifying each component of a game given in Section 7.1 are followed, students should be able to put things back in their containers correctly, and it is a good idea to add a section to the instructions for play asking them to check the contents of each container that they have taken materials from and to report any missing pieces to the teacher in charge.

None of these precautions will absolutely guarantee that the games kept in a resources centre (or a staff room) will remain in perfect order, but they will help keep administration time spent on materials to a minimum. One member of staff should be asked to take overall responsibility for doing running repairs and replacing missing pieces. Staff should report any damage or losses, having temporarily removed the affected games, which should be kept together on a separate shelf until the problem has been dealt with. A weekly checking and repair session should be enough to keep most collections of games in usable condition.

Language useful for playing and organising games

Equipment
a die/dice
a spinner
a board
a card
a counter
a piece
a scoreboard

Phrases
It's my/your, etc, turn/go
Whose turn/go is it?
One point to your team
Sorry! You lose a point/life
What's the score?
You lose a life
You're out
Who's winning?
They're catching up
You've won!
The winners!
It's a draw

Play
a player
a partner
a team
a turn/go/move
a life/lives
a square
a winner/loser
a scorer
to win/lose
to score
to draw/tie
to catch up
to drop out
to be 'in'/'out'
to go 'out'
to move/make a move

Bibliography

Byrne D, 'Three Interaction Activities', in Holden 1978: 10–14.

Cripwell K, 'Communication Games 1', in Holden 1978: 51–3.

Diagram Group, The, *The Way to Play, the Illustrated Encyclopedia of the Games of the World,* (London: Corgi Books, 1977).

ELT Documents 'Concept 7–9, A Course in Language and Reasoning', in ELT Documents 73/5: 10–13

Gibbs G I, *Handbook of Games and Simulation Exercises,* (London: E & F N Spon Ltd, 1974).

Gibbs G I, *Dictionary of Gaming, Modelling and Simulation,* (London: E & F N Spon Ltd, 1978).

Geddes M and McAlpin J, 'Communication Games 2', in Holden 1978: 54–7.

Holden S, (Ed), *Visual Aids for Classroom Interaction,* (London: Modern English Publications, 1978).

Kerr J Y K, 'Games and Simulations in English Language Teaching', in ELT Documents 77/1: 5–10.

Kerr J Y K, 'Picture Cue Cards for Pair or Group Work', in Holden 1978: 42–7.

Nation I S P, 'The Combining Arrangement: Some Techniques', in Modern Language Journal Vol 61 No 3 1977: 89–91.

Rixon S, 'The Information Gap and the Opinion Gap', in English Language Teaching Journal Vol 33 No 2 1979: 104–6.

Rixon S, *Teacher's Notes* to Communication Games in a Language Programme (ELTI Film No 4), (London: British Council Printing and Publishing Department, 1979).

Rixon S, *Games for Practising English,* (London: The Macmillan Press Ltd, 1981).

Films

Activity Days in Language Learning, (British Council, 1977).
Communication Games in a Language Programme, (British Council, 1978).

Sources of games

Books

Byrne D and Rixon S, (Eds), *ELT Guide 1 : Communication Games,* (Slough: National Foundation for Educational Research, for the British Council, 1979).

Carrier M, and Centre for British Teachers, The, *Take Five,* (London: Harrap, forthcoming).

Dorry G N, *Games for Language Learning,* (New York, London: McGraw-Hill, 1966).

Lee W R, *Language Teaching Games and Contests,* (London: Oxford University Press, 1979).

Rogers J D, (Ed), *Group Activities for Language Learning,* (Singapore: Seameo Regional Language Centre Occasional Papers No 4, 1978).

Wright A, Betteridge D and Buckby M, *Games for Language Learning,* (Cambridge: Cambridge University Press, 1979).

Purpose-designed materials

Concept 7–9 (The Schools Council and E J Arnold and Sons). Unit 3, *Communication,* is a kit of communication games intended for language and conceptual development in primary-age children, particularly those for whom English is a second language.

Games for Practising English (S Rixon, The Macmillan Press Ltd, 1981). A pack of picture cards, word cards and a teacher's booklet describing over thirty different games. The notes explain how to organise the games, how many people can play at a time and why games are a valuable teaching method in the English language classroom. The notes on each game specify the structures, functions and vocabulary practised and show the teacher how the games can be adapted for learners at different stages.

Interaction Packs A–C (with teacher's handbooks· Donn Byrne, Modern English Publications). Each pack contains multiple copies of visuals suitable for group or pair games with a class of about thirty students. The teacher's book explains how to prepare and exploit the materials.

Jabberwocky (Longman). A game using word cards in which players compete to create and modify sentences.

Picture Cue Cards (J Y K Kerr, Evans, 1979). Packs of picture cards on different topics, eg jobs, clothing, with a teacher's handbook giving more than eighty games and activities that they can be used for. Very useful in that the activities are listed according to the language points they are designed to cover.

Sounds Right! a game of Phonetic Bingo for language learning (John and Marion Trim, Cambridge University Press, 1978). A kit consisting of six Bingo cards with pictures on them and eighty-four caller's word-and-picture cards. The game is based on minimal sound contrasts, and players have to identify the words they hear with the correct pictures on their Bingo cards.

Think Links (Edward de Bono, Direct Education Services). Picture and word cards with a handbook giving instructions for many different games, mostly based on finding conceptual links between objects or ideas. The materials are intended for first language use with small children, but the principles behind the games can be applied to all levels and ages of foreign and second language learners.

Verb Bingo (Nina Hajnal, Longman 1978). A set of Bingo cards with irregular verbs on them, plus large flash cards for the caller to use, so that the game can be played aurally or as a reading exercise.

Games that can be adapted

Boggle (Chad Valley). A spelling game in which small cubes with a letter on each face are thrown. The players compete to see who can make the most words within a time limit.

The Great Game of Britain (Hi Toys). A board game in which players simulate rail travel around Britain with the object of visiting places of interest. Reading a) instructions on Chance cards and b) descriptions of tourist attractions plays a large part in the game.

Guts (National Health Service Learning Resources Unit, Sheffield). A game in which players try to collect sequences of cards relating to stages in the digestive process. There is a reference chart from which players can take information about correct groups of cards during the game.

Happy Families (Oxfam). This set of cards is a variant of the traditional Happy Families pack, showing families from all parts of the world.

Learning to Reason (Piatnik Fun School, Vienna: Piatnik, 1971). A set of playing cards with primary shapes – circle, square, triangle – in different sizes and three different colours – yellow, blue, red. Games involving matching (eg colour to colour, shape to shape) can be played with them rather like Picture Dominoes, as well as memory games and guessing games.

The London Game (Hi Toys). A board game in which players simulate travel on the London Underground to visit places of interest. Similar to The Great Game of Britain in the type of language practice it gives.

Longman Resources Unit Games (Longman): Geography Games, Science Games, History Games. These games come in sets in booklet form, complete with teaching notes and background material. The games have to be cut out and prepared by the teacher. They are intended to teach subject matter to native-speaking secondary school students, but some have great potential for use in English for Special Purposes courses.

Monopoly (Waddington). A very well-known board game which will be familiar to many students. Players simulate the buying and selling of property, and the transactions built into the game make it very productive of talk and discussion.

Quiz Card Games (Waddington, 1978). Packs of playing cards on different topics. Each card has a different coloured picture and some general knowledge questions about the picture on it. The cards can be used for a number of games, involving making sets of cards by answering the questions correctly. Good for reading comprehension practice and widening knowledge of subject matter. Topics include Tour of Britain, Tour of London, Tour of Knowledge and Highway Code.

Rainbow Play Packs (Jackdaw Publications for Thames Television, 1976). Packs of colourful visual materials intended for young children, containing games and puzzles that are very useful for young language learners. Each pack is on a different topic, such as *On the Farm*, and *People at Work*.

Scrabble (Spears). This game is also internationally popular. Players compete to form words which interlock in crossword fashion, using small letter tiles on a board. It is very good for students who are able to use a dictionary or word-list with some confidence and who wish to build their vocabulary, but it can be rather slow-moving with non-native speakers.

Shake Words (Peter Pan Playthings). A set of die cubes with a letter on each face. Players compete to form words from the letters that are uppermost after each throw. More limited in scope than Scrabble, which makes it a much faster game for language learners.

Tell Me (Spears). A roulette-type wheel with letters rather than numbers is spun. Players have to shout out a word or phrase beginning with that letter, according to categories given on small cards, eg the name of a river or a film star. These cards are easy to supplement with topics relevant to students' interests and general knowledge.

Index

Games described in text are shown in italics

Essential Language Teaching Series

Teaching techniques for communicative English **Jane Revell**
Pronunciation skills **Paul Tench**
How to use games in language teaching **Shelagh Rixon**
Developing listening skills **Shelagh Rixon**
Teaching English writing **Anita Pincas**
Look here! Visual aids in language teaching **Betty Morgan Bowen**
Language learners and their errors **John Norrish**
Reading in the language classroom **Eddie Williams**
A language testing handbook **Andrew Harrison**
Beginning English with young children **Opal Dunn**
Developing English with young learners **Opal Dunn**
English for specific purposes **Chris Kennedy & Rod Bolitho**
Using readers in language teaching **Tricia Hedge**
Video, tv and radio in the English class **Barry Tomalin**
Drama activities for language learning **John Dougill**
Large classes **Rob Nolasco & Lois Arthur**
Using literature in language teaching **Jennifer Hill**